An
AXE
for the
FROZEN
SEA

T0348798

Also by Ben Palpant

A Small Cup of Light
Sojourner Songs: Poems
The Stranger: Poems
Letters from the Mountain
Honey from the Lion's Mouth
Pepin and the Magician
Contributor to *Every Moment Holy, Vol. 3*

BEN PALPANT grew up in Kenya, Africa, where he played barefooted with his friends and perfected the art of daydreaming. When his family returned to the United States, he spent his adolescence daydreaming. Now he daydreams and calls it part of the writing process. He graduated from Whitworth University and spent over 25 years in education. Palpant is a memoirist, a poet, and a storyteller.

Discover more at www.benpalpant.com.

"A book must be an axe for the frozen sea within us."

— *Franz Kafka*

AN AXE FOR THE FROZEN SEA
by Ben Palpant
Copyright © 2024 Rabbit Room Press

Published by:
RABBIT ROOM PRESS
3321 Stephens Hill Lane
Nashville, Tennessee 37013

ISBN 9781951872311

Cover design by Ben Palpant © 2024
Book design by Ben Palpant

An
AXE
for the
FROZEN
SEA

RABBIT ROOM
— PRESS —

Also from
RABBIT ROOM PRESS

GLAD & GOLDEN HOURS
by Lanier Ivester
Illustrations by Jennifer Trafton

EVERY MOMENT HOLY
VOLS. 1, 2, 3
by Douglas Kaine McKelvey
Illustrations by Ned Bustard

THE MAJOR & THE MISSIONARY
by Diana Glyer

UNDONE
by Philip Yancey

RABBIT ROOM
— PRESS —

www.RabbitRoom.com

To all the poets

CONTENTS

PREFACE

If you had told me, back when I was just a lad, that I would choose to spend much of my 40s in conversation with poets and, worse yet, writing poems myself, I would have kicked you in the shins and run for the hills. I don't think my boy-sized brain could have conceived of a worse insult. Then, I met a living poet. It happened this way:

I was a senior in high school, holding a paper plate in a potluck line next to a stranger. Because my mother taught me to be polite, I struck up a conversation.

"What do you do?" I asked.

"I'm a poet," he replied.

I thought he was pulling my leg, but his face said otherwise. No smirk. No glint in his eye. I thought every last poet was dead, pinned onto the pages of boring textbooks, but here was a living one standing next to me, speaking to me in my native tongue. I fled.

Then, years later, I faced a health crisis that radically impacted my cognition for an extended period of time. Calamity tends to open our hearts to poetry. During that season of my life, I could not track an argument in prose, but I could follow a line of poetry to where it disappeared in the grass. It became important to my physical and mental stability that I learn to stand still in my heart, to wait patiently until my mind could pick up where the next poetic line offered itself and follow it. In poetry, I found unexpected comfort and, strangely, clarity—at least, a kind of clarity, the kind that poetry offers in paradox and metaphor. Poetry offered me insights that drew me deeper into life, and, in particular, my life with Christ. Poetry drew me, as Aslan says in *The Last Battle*, "further up and further in."

All these years later, poetry has come to play a significant part in my walk with God, which is why I set out at the start of 2024 to meet as many poets as I could and to spend an hour with each one—not to pepper them with questions, but to have a conversation that would lead us both further up and further in.

Someone will query, "Why interview poets?" To which I answer that I believe the best poets practice seeing what most of us overlook or take for granted. They know how to honor the particularities of human existence, thereby opening our eyes to see ourselves, God, and all of His creation with greater clarity and appreciation—an appreciation that leads from praise to greater praise. Poets draw us to attention. They help us sit up and take note, leading us to the heart of things and beyond the heart of things.

In other words, I believe poets can help us become more human—as God intended. Poets, through the ordinary means of the written word, can give us glimpses of the eternal. That's why I wanted these interviews to be less about the questions and answers and more about the human interaction. I wanted them to read like two people trying to dig deeper into what it means to be human, two friends exploring why poetry matters for all of life.

I did not intend to collect these conversations into a book, but it became apparent rather early on that reading them next to each other would be a reinforcing and fulfilling experience. Each interview is interesting and fruitful, but together they strengthen and enrich one another.

The title for this book comes from my conversation with Mischa Willett who mentioned Franz Kafka's famous line, "A book must be an axe for the frozen sea within us." It stuck with me, and so I have decided to title the book what I hope it will become—an axe for the frozen sea. Starting with the sea that threatens to freeze inside me from time to time.

Over the years, poetry has helped break up the sea of ice in my heart, which makes poets, I suppose, axe-wielders. I don't mean to describe these poets as people who have weaponized their words—though some of them might embrace that description—I mean that they have chosen the more difficult work of changing hearts. Heart change always begins with the poet, of course, but out of change of heart, the mouth speaks.

You will quickly discover that the poets in this book do not always agree. Their convictions vary, as do their practices. One of the interesting convictions they share, however, is that poetry is more than mere self-expression. In our day and age, that's a helpful connecting thread running through the discourse. I think I can say this with certainty, as well, that they all agree with Eliot's famous line about writing poetry: "every attempt is a wholly new start, and a different kind of failure . . . And so each venture / is a new beginning, a raid on the inarticulate."

I will be asked why I included some poets and did not include others. How I wish I could say that I picked these poets for particular reasons. Alas, I can't. I started with four poets who lived within driving distance. They, in turn, suggested other poets and so the project evolved organically. These poets by no means represent an exhaustive list of anything. Some are more famous than others, but fame is no indicator of quality and only time will tell which poets will have a lasting impact. At the end of the day, the world is full of worthy poets. Find them. Learn from them.

Given a thousand possible ways to structure this book, I opted to organize these poets alphabetically. It allows them to speak to each other and to us without any orchestration on my part. I also have a Get Out Of Jail Free card which I find entirely convenient if anyone complains about the order.

The question asked by every undergraduate, "Is poetry still relevant?" is a worthy one. The answer these conversations give is a resounding, "Yes!" But how is poetry relevant? Well, the answer to that question is as varied as the poets themselves.

When I look over the broad landscape of society, I see a reawakening of interest in and writing of poetry. If I'm correct, we need the best poets—both the living and the dead—to guide us into a deeper relationship with God, with ourselves, and with the world. Li-Young Lee once said, "People who read poetry have heard about the burning bush, but when you write poetry, you sit inside the burning bush." We need poets whose souls are fully awake so that we might glimpse what they sense throbbing at the heart of all things.

As the story goes, St. Augustine, weary of writing one day, decided to get some fresh air and walk the beach. He had not walked far when he saw a boy dashing back-and-forth from the ocean to a tiny hole in the sand. Augustine called out, "Hey there, what are you doing?" The boy lifted a shell which he had been using to transport sea water and cried out, "I'm going to fit the entire sea into this tiny hole I have dug in the sand!" Augustine laughed aloud. Spreading his arms wide, he said, "You attempt the impossible, my son. You will never fit this magnificent sea into that little hole." The boy, apparently familiar with the great theologian's efforts, called back, "And you will never fit the Holy Trinity inside your head!"

Well, imagine that there were two boys instead of only one, or a boy and a girl. Would their success rate improve? Hardly, but it would be good sport to watch. I suppose that's what these conversations amount to in the end. It's just two people trying to spoon the ocean into a tiny hole for an hour or so, doing our darndest not to spill a single drop along the way.

If you are a poet, this book is for you. May it inspire, instruct, and strengthen you for the work God has given you to do. If you are not a poet, may it remind you that words matter, that poetry matters, and that you matter—not in that particular order. Most of all, may these conversations spur us on to call out to God who loves to answer, so that He will show us great and mighty things which we did not know (Jeremiah 33:3).

Ben Palpant
September 2024

SCOTT
CAIRNS

"I remember being a boy, maybe three or four years old . . . I walked out into a very crisp winter night, and closed the door behind me. I stood on the threshold, my little feet on the doorstep, and as I looked up into the starry sky I had this exhilarating sense of joy, of beauty. I said out loud, 'I love life!'"

—*Scott Cairns*

Scott Cairns lives in a modest house, the house of his childhood, a house his father built. It is as unpretentious and welcoming as those who call it home. Standing together in the kitchen, gazing at Puget Sound, I am struck by the spirit in this place, the same spirit that infuses his poetry— an open-handed generosity, a down-to-earth gentleness, a wry, disarming humor.

He leads me downstairs, into a sunroom lined with windows, and gives me first dibs on where I want to sit. I select the old loveseat built out of bamboo. He's drinking his coffee from a mug that says, "7 days without a pun makes one weak." Glancing around the room, I notice the unremarkable furniture, the shelf lined with plants, the children's box set of Beatrix Potter books—it all strikes me as incredibly unassuming. The observation that comes to mind could seem insulting, but I choose to make it anyway.

"You don't seem to take yourself too seriously," I suggest.

"Well, I guess going to a lot of poetry readings over the years, listening to other poets, I find myself thinking, 'You don't have to be that severe, dude.'" He grins. "So, yes, I usually open my poems with a joke and then, at some point, you know, I get a little more serious, and the irony falls away. If you were raised in this home as I was, irony was a requirement. And puns were also required. How did Naomi Shihab Nye put it? 'Answer, if you hear the words under the words...' That is very similar to what I have said endlessly to my students, which is, pay attention to the words within the words."

"Maybe you could help me understand what you mean by that."

"I've noticed," he says, "that the poems I love most are poems that I can keep reading and opening because, during a given reading, I will have seen a primary sense of the word, but then see how the secondary and tertiary senses also figure into it. This is mostly why I started learning Greek and why I'm trying to learn a little Latin. It's because, as you must know, the English language is the best language for poetry. It's a museum for almost all the other languages. And so the etymological hauntings within an English word—of its Greek or Latin roots—may not be so overt, but they're present. If you're attentive to those ghosts, the poem keeps opening for you. It's never the same poem with each reading. I want to make poems like that, poems that keep opening. We should be cognizant that writing poems isn't about saying what you think you know; it's really about constructing a scene of meaning-making—a field into which a reader can enter and make meaning with the poet. There really ought to be some ambiguity implicated in every line, I think."

"Does the ambiguity play into line breaks for you?" I ask. "How do you make decisions on line endings?"

"I am almost always counting something; that's one technical element of lineation. I also want my lines to register as a provisional, syntactical unit which is then modified by subsequent lines. Often, for instance, the word out here at the end of the line appears to be a noun, but then it turns out that it's an adjective modifying an actual noun waiting in the next line. That provides a wonderful, dizzying experience for the reader who then is obliged to take another look at what he just read, and his re-reading proves essential to the agency of what I like to call the poetic operation of language."

"Which is what we like about our favorite poems."

He nods and takes a drink from his mug. "Poetry," he says, "when it's really poetry, occasions this sort of spinning, vertiginous—I like the word vertiginous—

operation of language. You can also witness this in a rich prose text. Poetry, of course, can happen in verse or prose. Even fiction, nonfiction, and drama can obtain some degree of this poetic operation of language—this delicious, puzzling, opening activity. A great novel like Fyodor Dostoevsky's *The Brothers Karamazov*—a book I read every summer—does this. It keeps opening me onto something new."

He pauses and gazes out the window. "I really do feel that when I'm making a poem, it's not about having a glimpse of something true and then trying to transcribe it. It's more like trying to figure it out, glimpsing it as I go, wrestling with the language, listening to the music of the words, letting the music lead me to the next words. And in that way, my compositional practice is also my meditation." He thinks for a moment. "I guess for the first half of my life I resisted the equation between poetry and prayer. Over the past twenty years, however, I have approached my poems as a kind of prayer—perhaps my most efficacious prayer."

"It sounds to me like your favorite poets force you to calibrate to mystery," I say, "but that's also partly why you write. You're calibrating to the divine mystery."

"Well, yes, because I'm my first audience. I want to get something out of it, too." He laughs. "You should know that I really only have five ideas. I think they're pretty good ideas, but to the extent that ideation occurs in any of my poems ever, they're pretty much the same five ideas retooled, if opening a little more onto a fuller glimpse each time I work it over. One of the hardest things for young readers to figure out is that there really is no hidden code in the poem. The reader's purpose is not to crack the code and replace the poem with a paraphrase of the poem. No, a genuine poem is actually a place you enter and experience, a place in which you collaborate in meaning-making."

While he takes another drink from his mug, I consider the room around me quietly before beginning my thought. "When I drove up to your house today," I say, "I thought of your house as just a house."

"A very modest house," he replies.

"But when you told me that your dad built this house, my perspective shifted. In a way, I walked through this house differently. It seems as though poems, if we think of them as a place, should be entered with a different kind of respect. I'm not just entering an apartment that is produced *en masse*, I'm entering a place that had a great deal of meaning long before I entered it."

"Ah, a dwelling place," he suggests.

"Yes. How do you enter a poem with that kind of respect?"

"Well," he says, "I suppose, when I start reading, I'm not looking for any inspiration, anything to take. I'm just ingesting the page, you know. If it draws me back later, if I keep going back to the poem again and again, then something grows out of that thorough reading. It's the poets like W. H. Auden, C. P. Cavafy, that I come back to. Do you know Cavafy? He was a Greek poet living in Alexandria, Egypt in the early twentieth century. He's a fantastic poet. I have certain other favorites—Mark Strand, Anthony Hecht. Anyway, I spend a lot of time with them, you see. They become sort of my primary audience. They write to me, I write to them. Richard Howard was one of my beloved mentors, one of the best-read guys I've met. I pore over the works of these people and hope that some of it rubs off. I end up writing to satisfy them more than to satisfy, I don't know, the living."

He continues, "I want students to be less concerned with what the author is saying and more concerned with what they can literally make with the poem on the page. The entire literary history is really all about a conversation that has been going on for centuries. To be part of that conversation, first you have to read to find out what that conversation is, and let the utterances of other writers provoke your responses. The more you're equipped by the prior discourse, the more likely you are to make something interesting with it, something that might actually contribute to the ongoing conversation."

"Let's talk about calibrating to mystery," I say. "During difficult times of life, do you find yourself writing more? Or less?"

"It has probably varied over the years," he replies. "As an escape from the turmoil, yes. Sometimes just saying, 'To heck with it, I'm going to work on this poem,' is a great thing. Other times, things are going well and I still get the legal pad out and start reading again. Most of my writing time, you see, begins with reading time. I'll be poring over a book and, eventually, I glimpse something new. My legal pad and number two pencils are out and ready, so I start responding to whatever glimpse I just had. I start looking for more openings onto new glimpses in this new work. So there's this linguistic dynamic at work that continues to give, to push me, to open me."

"Do you leave unfinished poems out and about so they're always calling to you?"

"You saw my desk." He chuckles. "I think that would qualify as out and about. At some point, I'll move them to the laptop."

"You strike me as a poet who isn't under some delusion that he's arrived," I say. "There's always something to pursue, to learn."

"The older I get, the more I feel I have to achieve and the more I feel like I'm not going to make it, that I'm going to run out of time." He laughs. "That's pretty much a guarantee."

"Do you feel the weight that John Keats felt when he had fears that he may cease to be . . . when he beheld cloudy symbols that he may never live to trace their shadows? Do you feel that?"

"I have always been cognizant of death, but it's a little more present as I age, yes. But I think of Samuel Coleridge; he was always trying to mine something. I've found his continual reaching to be compelling. I never want to give in to the notion that if something comes easily I should keep doing that thing."

"How have you wrestled with public praise?" I ask. "How have you kept it from warping your work?"

"I guess I avoid it as much as possible," he says before taking another sip. "I've never been good at taking compliments. Maybe it's just part of my deflecting humor. One of the best ways to defend against its poor effect upon one's character is to know some genuinely brilliant people. It keeps you humble. Of course, I also have friends who don't read poetry at all. I don't think it's for everyone. I think you need to have a taste for uncertainty, which is a taste I think most people don't share. Most people are profoundly burdened by practical matters. They may feel that they have no room for uncertainty, but that feeling keeps them from discovering, keeps them from a deep species of joy. Uncertainty is a great gift. I think uncertainty is a truer disposition than certainty. For instance, God is not reducible to anything we can say about God. God necessarily always exceeds what we might make of God; so, too, the truth necessarily always exceeds what we can narrowly define. If we think we can enclose the truth—or enclose God—we're not talking about truth and we're not talking about God."

"Could we take a moment to talk about the next generation of writers? What are some of the missteps you see young writers taking?"

"The only time I really get distressed about my students," he replies, "is when marketing and self-promotion starts taking up too much of their attention and time. I think self-promotion is a really bad idea for a couple of reasons—the greatest of which is that you start thinking that public attention is how you know your work is good. Applause and acclaim are not how you know something has quality. Witnessing all the self-promotion they're doing, I feel very sad. I start to wonder if maybe I forgot to say something to them when I had the chance, something important."

"Are you suggesting," I ask, "that the market economy has no overlap with poetry?"

"No, marketing has a place, but the poet shouldn't be the one to do it. The poet should have some really great friends who love to share his work with other people."

"So he can focus on the work?"

"Truly, yes, just do the work. I'm not saying you shouldn't send your work out for publication, but I spend probably an hour a month thinking about what I have on hand to send out, and who I should send it to. Then I send it off and forget about it—I get back to work. That seems to me a healthy ratio. But more than that, I think that a daily Instagram post about your deep thoughts doesn't seem like a good use of your deep thoughts. I don't get angry about marketing; I don't get resentful. And yes, I think writers really do get noticed that way, but I just mostly feel sad for folks who get swept up in it."

"You wrote a book called *Idiot Psalms*. One of my personal favorites is 'Psalm 2, a psalm of Isaak accompanied by baying hounds.' Who is Isaak?"

"There actually was a Saint Isaak of Syria. He was a seventh-century monastic who was bishop for about three hours before he fled back to the desert. I first came upon him while reading *The Brothers Karamazov*. One of the characters is said to have read the *Ascetical Homilies of Saint Isaac the Syrian* nearly every day, understanding none of it. So that's the actual Saint Isaak. When I became Orthodox, I took the name Isaak; he is my 'name saint,' as we say. Now, when I take communion, they don't call me Scott, they call me Isaak. So these poems, and others of mine, are understood to be spoken by a persona, Isaak the Least."

"Would you read the poem?"

O Shaper of varicolored clay and cellulose, O Keeper
       of same, O Subtle Tweaker, Agent
       of energies both appalling and unobserved,
       do not allow Your servant's limbs to stiffen
       or to ossify unduly, do not compel Your servant
       to go brittle, neither cramping at the heart,
       nor narrowing his affective sympathies
       neither of the flesh nor of the alleged soul.

Keep me sufficiently limber that I might continue
       to enjoy my morning run among the lilies

and the rowdy waterfowl, that I might
delight in this and every evening's intercourse
with the woman you have set beside me.

Make me to awaken daily with a willingness
to roll out readily, accompanied
by grateful smirk, a giddy joy,
the idiot's undying expectation,
despite the evidence.

"Thank you," I say. "I love that final stanza so much that I wrote it down in my journal several years ago so I could look at it regularly."

"Well, I wrote what I hope for myself, you know. The evidence is not promising, but there is a grace in supposing that despite how unpromising the surrounding evidence—the circumstances of our political lives, our civic lives, our individual progress towards holiness—there is an inescapable deep note of joy that I've been blessed with and count on."

"What a gift," I reply.

"I remember being a boy—maybe three or four years old—and we were getting ready to visit my grandmother's house," he says. "I was ready early because I didn't have much to do, and so I walked out into a very crisp winter night, and closed the door behind me. I stood on the threshold, my little feet on the doorstep, and as I looked up into the starry sky I had this exhilarating sense of joy, of beauty. I said out loud, 'I love life!' You know, the expression of an earnest young person. But that has stuck with me. It was this huge blessing, this realization that it's all okay, now and ever. It was a moment that set me up for resistance against the despair that would woo me later in life."

Imperative
by Scott Cairns

The thing to remember
is how tentative all of this
really is. You could wake up dead.

Or the woman you love
could decide you're ugly.
Maybe she'll finally give up
trying to ignore the way you
floss your teeth when
you watch television.
All I'm saying is that
there are no sure things here.

I mean, you'll probably wake up alive,
and she'll probably keep putting off
any actuall decision about your looks.
Could be she'll be glad your teeth
are so clean. The morning could be
full of all the love and kindness
you need. Just don't go thinking
you deserve any of it.

ROBERT CORDING

"I never felt angry at the loss of my son because I don't believe God took my son's life as a destructive act. God is always making. That's what he does continually. And I believe that at the heart of life is the choice to embrace God's work, even at great personal cost. My work as a poet, my relationships, my daily decisions depend upon embracing the God who makes and will always make as an overflow of love."

—*Robert Cording*

L et me put all my cards on the table here and just admit, up front, that I chose to interview Robert Cording not primarily because he is a first-rate Christian poet (which he is), but because he entered the abyss called grief and his poetry testifies to the one whom he found at the bottom: God. The word "testify" is, perhaps, not quite right. I mean to say that his poetry *sings* of God. He is like a bird caught in a well, a well that we sidestep as long as possible, but which we all must fall down sooner or later. I suppose another way to put it is that I chose to interview Cording because I want his company when that day arrives. I chose him because he would remind me that nothing can separate us from the love of God (Romans 8:38-39). Not even grief.

Cording opens his latest book of poems with a quote from the Greek philosopher Epicurus: "Against other things it is possible to obtain security, but when it comes to death, we human beings all live in an unwalled city." Cording is an unwalled city and he knows it. That's perhaps all I need to say by way of introduction, but I'll say this, too: He is no graveside haunt. Instead of a pale, morose aspect, his is rosy and sun-kissed. Instead of getting strung out on the opium of despair, Cording is clear-eyed and hopeful. He would be the first to demystify his title as poet, to tell you that he is just a regular guy who lost his son like so many before him. He would be the first to say that when it comes to his poetry, he's just trying to say what he doesn't know how to say.

Right out of the gate, I confess my intentions to Cording. "You should know that I have a singular plan for you," I say. He laughs. "My other interviews touch here and there on grief, but none of them stays on the subject very long. You strike me as a man who is willing to sit in uncomfortable spaces. Why don't you start by telling me about your son?"

"Happily. Well, let's see. We lost our son six years ago, in October. Daniel had terrible back problems for five years. The discs in his spine were disintegrating, so he would have these spasms that put him on the ground and he couldn't walk. He was young, late twenties when it started, and had been a very good athlete, so they didn't want to fuse his back. Instead, they decided to shave away the extrusions. To deal with the pain, they prescribed him opioids. He definitely became addicted to them. He knew it. The doctor knew it. But they didn't stop prescribing them because it was the only way to deal with the pain. He died of an accidental drug overdose. The more important thing is not his death, but his life. He graduated with a degree in philosophy and architecture, did a summer program at Harvard in architectural design, and started his own business refurbishing houses. His work was very physical. I know I'm biased, but the thing that made Daniel extraordinary was that he took the question 'Why?' seriously, and he never settled for easy answers."

"He was a thinker."

"Yes, and in a way his death offered no easy answers. You know, we don't know how to make sense of death. We can't move past it or get around it, so we have to embrace it. I know it sounds strange to say it that way, but I truly believe that if we don't embrace death in the way that we should embrace joy—as an inexplicable thing—then we harm ourselves. We end up mourning eternally for something that we can't have again. The only defense we have against death, if you want to call it a defense—I would call it an offense, myself—is love. Solomon says that love is as strong as death. I believe that remembrance is a way to love. That's why I started writing about him. Writing is an act of love and an act of remembrance. It seems to me a necessity to make Daniel a daily part of my life, just as he was when he was alive."

"You're leaning into love as much as possible."

"Yes. You can't sidestep anything when you do that, and you have to accept what happens to you. You know, some of us are tempted to control every circumstance so that nothing bad ever happens to us, but that way of living always collapses on itself. Those kinds of people are always unhappy. We just don't have control over much in life. We have control over our own actions, of course, but not much more than that. We have to embrace those things that are out of our control. Leaning into love means doing more than accepting Daniel's death, hard as that is. It means holding the grief as closely as I can. It means not protecting myself from grief but making the grief as intimate as possible. It allows me to hold him close, even in death. We have to embrace the loss in order to embrace our son most fully."

"I was talking to a young person the other day who said that she had worked her whole life to evade trouble, to control her circumstances, but it always seemed to find her. She said that she had entered a very dark place, but affirmed that it was when God took away her control, when he put her in the very place she dreaded most, that's when he met her there. All she had left was God. That seems to me to illustrate what you're talking about."

"It does very much. I'm reminded of John 16:7 where Jesus tells his disciples that he must go away so that they might be comforted. I'm not sure how to explain that, except to say that maybe the Holy Spirit, the comforter, gives us a presence inside the absence. When I embraced Daniel's absence, I felt comforted."

"You bring up the Holy Spirit's work in your life. I'm wondering what his role is for you as a poet. Do you see the Holy Spirit as the equivalent of what the ancients referred to as the Muse?"

"I do. I think one of the things we've lost is the invocations that the older writers used to make before they wrote. The first time I went through The Spiritual Exercises of Saint Ignatius, I worked with my friend, Father MacDonald, who said at the start that we would invoke the Holy Spirit so that maybe something could happen here. With just the two of us, we needed some help." He laughs. "I really feel that way about my writing. Poetry is always trying to see beyond what we can see. We know that's impossible and yet we can, as Scripture says, see through a glass darkly. We know more than we can say. Every act of writing is also a failure to say what we most want to say, but it is an attempt. It's an attempt to describe what it means to be alive in this world. The seminal experience of my life is that I live in a world that's good, but so many bad things happen in it. And yet, I've never lost the sense that the world was good at its core. For me, everything begins with Genesis 1."

"It seems to me that your poetry has always pointed to the goodness of creation in some way."

"Yes, I would say that it's the touchstone of all my writing. I was lucky enough to find my obsession in college. It happened in a funny way. My mother, who thought I was just in a dreary mood because I wore so much dark clothing, wanted me to be happier. She told me to sit down and write a list of all the bad things in life on one side of a paper and then write all the good things on the other side. So I did. Being the person that I was, I began with the bad things. This was in the late '60s, with racism, the Vietnam War, a seemingly endless list. But when I got to about thirty or forty items, I had this incredible realization. If I can list all of these bad things, why do I have this abiding sense that life is still good? I really did feel that life was, in the end, good. I've spent the rest of my life writing about that sense of goodness at the core of things."

"You're reminding me of my conversation with Paul Mariani, who said that his hero, Gerard Manley Hopkins, just wanted to write at God's dictation, to hear the Holy Spirit as clearly as possible and for his poetry to reflect clearly what he heard. That seems to me to be where you find yourself."

"Yes. My favorite poet is George Herbert. For Herbert and Hopkins and myself, the dilemma is that maybe we love the language we use to describe God more than we love God. This was the dilemma I ran into when writing about my son as well. I wanted *In The Unwalled City* to be more than a book about grief; I wanted it to be artistic. I wanted it to be beautiful. That sounds crass, perhaps, to write something artistic about your son who died, but there it is. I did want to write something that was crafted, that was beautifully written. I wanted something more than diary entries or spilling my heart on the page. As a result, the book is highly structured. I think if I'm going to move people in any significant way, I must move them by the artistry and not just the sentiment."

"Andrew Peterson says that the job of the Christian artist is to adorn the dark. That's what you're doing in this book. You're trying to adorn your son's life and his memory in a way that doesn't feel gaudy or artificial, but in a way that honors him best."

"And it requires a grateful heart to do that," he adds.

"Yes, it does."

"But that's exactly what I felt cut off from when Daniel died. This was true for two years. It was hard to be grateful. All my life, I have felt that gratefulness equals a kind of contentment. I think that's true, but it was just not within reach for a while. My wife and I would take a walk every day and I don't think she looked up for six months. Finally, one day we took a walk, and I saw two hawks doing this aerial display, a kind of mating ritual, and I said to her, 'You have to look at this. It's unbelievable.' After that, the natural world helped us live again. William Wordsworth felt this keenly. He's one of my favorites because he felt like the natural world could help in more ways than we know, including helping us be better people. I believe that, too. Like Hopkins, I believe that every moment of every day, the world shows us the 'grandeur of God.'"

"This must have an effect on your choice of poetic form. Your work is eclectic in its forms, but I'm wondering how you choose. You know, a sonnet is a lovely way of artistically making a point, but it might not be the most effective way to express our deepest passions, whether rage or utter exaltation and joy."

"I never actually think about the form initially. Whenever I've written a sonnet, it actually started out as something else until I realized that there was a sonnet there that the poem was asking to become. For me, writing about grief was a matter of bringing in voices—prose voices, formal poetry voices, raw poetry voices that are uninhibited, and my son's voice, too. I wanted my son to speak. I think he has the best lines in the book."

"Did you have poets that ministered to you in times of grief?"

"Yes. Herbert's poem, 'The Bag,' begins this way:

Away despair! my gracious Lord doth heare.
Though windes and waves assault my keel,
He doth preserve it: he doth steer,
Ev'n when the boat seems most to reel.
Storms are the triumph of his art:
Well may he close his eyes, but not his heart.

Reading that poem, I realized that, yes, I too must not close my heart. If Christ would not close his heart, then why should I? No matter how difficult the grief, you must not close your heart."

"To close one's heart is a self-destructive act," I say.

"Yes."

"Do you find that, if we are honest, sometimes we want to destroy ourselves in times of grief, to close our eyes, even literally and permanently? Maybe we want to put ourselves on some kind of pyre rather than face naked grief."

"Indeed," he says. "But Christ did not close his eyes."

"No, he did not," I reply. "Your words remind me of when Christ appeared to the disciples after he rose from the dead. Thomas, in particular, was a man like me, a skeptic, a man whose grief accentuated his skepticism. In my opinion, skepticism was a way of shielding himself against pervasive loss. Christ doesn't just say, 'Look, here I am.' Christ invites Thomas to put his hand in Christ's side. It's a kind of invitation to embrace death fully, to really come to grips with what happened."

"I agree," he says. "It's an invitation to be fully human, to face death, and, as a result, the incomprehensibility of resurrection. In Wordsworth's 'Peele Castle,' a poem about his brother who drowned at sea, he says that the death of his brother humanized his soul. I think that's really true, but only if we embrace death as we ought to embrace it. The grief actually makes us more human, more compassionate, more attentive to our connections with each other."

"It seems to me that you can spot a kinship rather quickly with someone who has suffered deeply."

"Yes, it's true. As a teacher, I was always very moved by students who had suffered terrible things at an early age. I felt a deep compassion. I'll tell you something about when Daniel died. Whether it was a good parenting decision or not, I told my other two sons that we were going to go down to the funeral home to be with Daniel after he died. I wanted them to see their brother before the funeral home doctored him up, before they changed him to be more fit for public viewing. So we went, the three of us, and sat with Daniel for over an hour. I told them we were going to stay with Daniel's body until we had grown comfortable with death, as comfortable as we can become. We wanted to honor him by letting his death imprint itself on our bodies. I made my sons touch their brother's face. Six years later, they say that they are really grateful for that experience."

"Your story reminds me of Nikos Kazantzakis," I say. "His autobiography, *Report to Greco*, is really wonderful. I'll never forget one moment in his childhood when war broke out and flooded the streets. They bolted the door and sat against the wall, listening through the night to the sound of bloodshed. In the morning, when life began again, his father took him into the streets to show little Nikos the dead. At one point, they came to three men who had been hanged. His father made him touch and kiss their feet. The difference between your story and this Kazantzakis story, at least as it seems to me, is that his father was saying to Nikos, 'This is reality, get used to it.' But yours was an act of faith."

"The first person who died in my life was my great-grandmother. I was very afraid, sitting in church, knowing that she was dead in the coffin at the front of the church. When it was time, my mother marched me all the way up to the front of the church and took my hand and placed it on my great-grandmother's cheek and on her lips and then on her forehead. My mother told me that I would always have the touch of her. It was a kind of gift, a kind of embracing death rather than simply facing it."

"At one point in the book you quote Henry James, who said that we work in the dark. Could you unpack that for me, especially in terms of writing poetry?"

"I've always believed that we live in a world that is untranslatable, unexplainable, but intelligible. That's the part everyone leaves out when they talk about mystery. They talk about mystery as if it will one day no longer be a mystery when we have all of the facts, but there is no accounting for most things, actually. Most sacred mysteries are beyond our grasp, but that doesn't mean they're unapproachable or unintelligible. That's why we can have the gifts of physics and mathematics, all the disciplines we teach. But when we're writing poetry, we're trying to approach mystery through intelligible things. As a poet, you try to move as close to mystery as you possibly can. Poetry allows us to do what rational arguments don't," he says. "Poetry is especially suited to this because it uses images. Robert Frost says that poetry says one thing in terms of another. In poetry something can mean two things at once, sometimes paradoxically. This is often how we experience life—like suffering and joy—but poetry makes that which seems beyond reason intelligible and rational. It helps to make a kind of sense out of our experience."

"Ephesians 2:10 says that we are God's *poiema*. How have you thought of that word in the context of grief?"

"The word literally means workmanship, something made. God has made us. God has made everything. Just think of the planet we live on, spinning as it does at such a velocity through space. God made it spin in such a way that we don't fly off of it. And it remains just at the right distance from the sun so that we neither fry nor freeze. The only explanation for this exactness is divine love. That's where the word 'workmanship' comes into play. When Moses climbed the mountain to receive the Ten Commandments, the Israelites made a golden calf. They made it because they were afraid. But when God tells them to make the Ark of the Covenant, they make it out of love."

"That's an interesting distinction."

"Well, I believe that God wants us to make like he makes, from an overflow of love. Christians, especially, ought to make out of love. You know, I never felt angry at the loss of my son because I don't believe God took my son's life as a destructive act. God is always making. That's what he does continually. And I believe that at the heart of life is the choice to embrace God's work, even at great personal cost. My work as a poet, my relationships, my daily decisions depend upon embracing the God who makes and will always make as an overflow of love."

Larches
by Robert Cording

The green-gone-to-gold larches gilded
my view for three weeks, but now
these deciduous evergreens slough off
their needles that lie in a ring beneath
the trees. Already I miss their feathery tops
tempering the wind of a pop-up storm
as if there was something like a calm
kindness at the heart of things.

Now the dark comes early, pools
under the larches and keeps on rising
until the darkness of the trees seek
each other. I wait for the dark to rise up
in me as if it's my duty. I believe,
as much as I can, that the sorrow
arriving each evening is the hard gift
required of me. I have stood here

so many evenings, my sorrow
has become its own relief. So I wait
for the stab of love and its wound
of remembering my dead son
who I must keep from becoming the ghost
of all I do not remember. His death is
a different death, unlike the larches
that do not need me to bring back their life.

DANA
GIOIA

"Having spent my life in huge cities—in major universities, corporations, and public institutions—I had developed a delusional sense of my own importance. That subjectivity was slowly eroded by witnessing the objective reality of the world. Wisdom seemed to know my small piece of the natural world as well as I could. And to love and protect it. I didn't need to think about God when I could feel him everywhere around me."

—*Dana Gioia*

Even though Dana Gioia no longer serves as chairman of the National Endowment for the Arts or California's poet laureate, he's still a busy man in high demand. So when he called, I expected a ten-minute business meeting and pulled the car to the side of a busy road. What I got instead was an energized, friendly, and informative conversation that took over an hour before we ever got on topic. I learned more about opera in that time than I have learned in my entire life (yes, you can call me a philistine), but mostly it was story after story that made us lose track of time. When we finally decided that we should get to the topic, I pitched him my idea.

"Look," I said, "I don't pretend to care more about your work than you do, but the twenty acres that you call home in California is conspicuously absent in your interviews.

It's mentioned, but never really explored. But I have a hunch that it's important to you."

The phone went quiet and I thought I had lost connection or, even worse, made a terrible suggestion. I decided to fill the void. "If that's true, then it would be a disservice to your readers and a major gap in the documentation of your life if it was never talked about in detail."

Silence, and then his voice: "Ben," he said, "I love that idea. This property has had an outsized impact on me, and nobody asks me about it. Come with me." I heard the gravel crunching beneath his feet as he walked down a path. "We need to check on my bluebird nest. The wild fires over the last few years have severely damaged the bird population, and I'm trying to rehabilitate it." We talked for another twenty minutes. I told him about the spotted towhee nest I found the other day, built at the base of a tree. He told me about the doe that comes when called (she's named Betty). The conversation had already begun.

So when we picked up where we left off several weeks later, I asked him to tell me the story of his journey to this beautiful place, starting with his childhood in Southern California.

"I was born and raised in Los Angeles," he says. "We lived in a stucco apartment building set among other apartments. There were no front yards, only concrete driveways. Across the street were the garbage cans of businesses along Hawthorne Boulevard—a liquor store, a Chinese restaurant, and a mortuary. My world was entirely urban. There was no open land. The parks were small and spare. I saw nothing natural except the beach and the Pacific Ocean, so my sense of nature was huge, wet, and inhuman. Both of my parents worked multiple jobs. We never took vacations longer than a weekend. I never saw a forest until I was twelve."

"But you've shared elsewhere that you had a good childhood," I reply.

"My childhood was happy. I had good parents. Our family of six was surrounded by relations, many of whom lived in the apartments around us. I took my daily world for granted. Yet I had a small but constant sense of deprivation, a hunger for beauty that expressed itself in my excessive reactions to art and brief glimpses of nature."

"When did you first come into contact with the natural world?" I ask.

"Except for the beach, my first real encounters with nature began in college. I went north to Stanford, which fifty years ago still had a rural setting—now entirely gone due to the overbuilding of Silicon Valley and the campus itself. There were oak woods between the campus and Palo Alto. Behind the campus were open hills. I wandered through the woods and hills nearly every day. When political protests shut down the campus, a girl invited me to go camping in the coastal range. We took sleeping bags without any gear. We slept on the beach or in the woods. We rarely saw another human being. I felt as if I were on a different planet."

"Did those college experiences change you?"

"Very little. I loved the open land, but I considered myself an urban animal. I thought I could never live anywhere except a major city—L.A., New York, Washington, San Francisco. I spent two years at Harvard and hated Boston. I thought it was mostly the weather, but perhaps it was the first inkling of change. After returning to California for business school, I moved to New York. I spent the next twenty years in Westchester County, just north of Manhattan. I thrived in New York's milieu, but it never felt like home. Yet I stayed. I was successful in both the business and literary world. I had no external motivation to leave."

"And yet you did leave. Why? Did something unsettle you?"

"While I was in business school, my parents left Los Angeles. My father had been robbed twice at gunpoint. One of his friends had been killed. My folks felt that they had to get out of their neighborhood. My father had never lived anywhere but Los Angeles and Detroit, but he fostered a fantasy about living in a small town. My mother, who had lived in Hawthorne all her life, also longed to go somewhere else. They bought a house on an old chicken farm in Sebastopol, sixty miles north of the Golden Gate Bridge. Sonoma County was still rural then. They were surrounded by apple orchards. I started going up to see them on weekends. Once in New York, I came out several times a year. I spent my vacations visiting them. I helped them with their small orchard and my mother's tiny organic fruit and herb business. I began to think of this new place as home."

"A stark contrast to your daily life at the time," I suggest. "Did you ever imagine moving there?"

"Moving there was unrealistic," he replies. "I couldn't make a living. I was tied to metropolitan cities."

"What changed in your life that let you leave your big city existence?" I ask.

"In 1992, at the age of forty-one, I quit my job at Kraft — General Foods. I had become a well-known poet. My essay 'Can Poetry Matter?' had made an international impression. I felt I could make a living writing. For the next four years, despite some ups and many downs, I managed to support my family."

"I'm sure you felt a sense of freedom."

"I was vastly relieved to leave corporate life, but I still felt out of place in New York. My wife loved Westchester County, especially our charming, ramshackle village, Hastings-on-Hudson. The New York metro area was the best place for a writer. Leaving made no career sense."

"Moving made no sense, and yet you moved. Why?"

"While visiting my parents, we saw a house for sale and decided—then and there—to buy it. I wasn't in the market for a house. I had not intended to move. It was the only place we looked at. Yet as I put my foot on the ground from the car, I knew this was where I would live. It was an irrational but irrefutable feeling. I needed to change my life, and it would happen here."

"That's quite a revelation."

"The trouble was that we couldn't afford the house. I kept talking to the owner. There was a property slump in California. Nothing was selling. After six months of offers and counter-offers, we bought it with a massive mortgage. We moved there in early January of 1996 with two small kids, a cat, no money, and no local employment. It rained every day for two weeks."

"That's a tough start. Was the adjustment difficult?" I ask. "I imagine that the change in noise levels alone would have taken acclimatization."

"It was an enormous shock. I had no idea of what it meant to live in the country. Back then we could hardly see another light at night, even though we were on top of a hill. The coastal fog would drift in and leave us in isolation. My first night I couldn't sleep. Every sound alarmed me. And the dark woods around us were full of noises—owls, coyotes, foxes, and deer. You could hear animals moving in the trees and brush. Sounds of savage battles would erupt as packs of coyotes attacked the flocks of wild turkeys."

"People often dream of moving into the country," I add, "but they don't reckon with these kinds of adjustments."

"Having spent my life in L.A. and New York, I also felt vulnerable to human danger, although it was unlikely anyone would drive up the steep country road to rob us. It took me a few weeks to shed my urban anxiety."

"With less light pollution, you probably saw a more vibrant night sky."

"One of the things that shocked me most when I came here was the moon. I realized I'd never truly seen it before. In Los Angeles or New York, it is a pale, diminished thing lost in the haze of city lights. But in the country, the moon ruled the night. A full moon lit my way through the woods and fields. When it was down, night was black. What poet two hundred years ago would have been so ignorant?

"Tell me about the property. What do you see as you walk it—the geology, the shape of the land?"

"We bought twenty acres, very little of which is flat. Our write farm house is on the top of a hill with no other house nearby. The property slopes downhill in every direction. We look down to the floor of the Sonoma Valley which, at that time, was all vineyards, ranches, and horse farms."

"What's the soil like?"

"The ground is extraordinarily stony. Some glacier had carved the small canyon next to us and deposited all its Ice Age debris. When we plant trees, we have to dig the pit and remove the rocks—there are more rocks than soil."

"What trees grow in that kind of soil?"

"The hillsides were covered with black oaks, coast live oaks, and white oaks mixed in with madrones, pines, and buckeyes. The black oaks were enormous trees, hundreds of years old. Some redwoods grew in the pockets where the night fogs gathered. The whole area was thickly wooded. I decided I wouldn't plant anything that wasn't native to the area."

"What do you mean, it was thickly wooded?"

"We lost over half the trees in the Kincade fire of 2019, one of half a dozen massive wildfires that raged through Sonoma, Napa, and Lake counties. This fire alone burned 78,000 acres. Few of the old oaks survived, and almost none of the pines. My forest turned into lightly wooded hillsides and meadows. It took us four years to clear out the dead trees. I planted dozens of oaks and nurtured the natural reforestation. Seeing that horrible destruction and nature's response was an illumination."

"What else was on your property? What sort of wildlife?"

"When we first got here, we couldn't have told you what was on our property. My wife and I had been raised in cities. We didn't know the names of things. Coming here made me realize how alienated we were from the natural world. We decided that we would learn the names of all the plants and animals in our locale."

"That's a noble aim. I'm afraid I wouldn't know where to start."

"We learned the trees first. There were really only about a dozen varieties. Then we learned the birds. We have acorn woodpeckers, Steller's jays, scrub jays, ravens, turkeys, quail, vultures, spotted towhees, northern flickers, red-tailed hawks, and great-horned owls, to name only the larger birds. My wife became so interested that she became a serious birder."

"What about the plants and flowers?"

"The plants are more challenging. We learned the wildflowers, but their weedy companions were harder to master, though many have colorful names—coyote bush, miner's lettuce, foxtail, quaking grass, and umbrella sedge. Knowing the names of plants changed my relationship to the landscape and the seasons. Wild grasses and thistles grow thigh-high in the spring with yarrow, spearmint, and sage. When the plants die, we have to cut them for fire protection. It takes months of work to keep the place safe."

"Did living on that property change you in any fundamental way as a person?" I ask.

"Living here gradually changed me in so many ways that it is hard to explain the process. I went from a very social urban life to a very solitary rural one."

"You were alone with your thoughts."

"My property bordered on other open land. I often finished an outside chore and decided to walk through the woods. I had never lived in woodlands. I had just been a tourist. I had never hiked so much alone. I tramped around in all sorts of weather, and got lost in both the landscape and my thoughts. I realized I had a deep need for solitude and contemplation. I had been starved in my previous life. If you spend hours every day in solitude and quiet observation, it transforms you."

"Did it change you as a Christian?"

"More deeply than I ever expected. I had always been a very intellectual Catholic. My education had filled me with theology, philosophy, and church history. I thought my way through religion. Living in a natural landscape across the seasons, I watched the world move forward without human agency. Everything had a shape and purpose that mysteriously unfolded around me. I had never viscerally understood the notion of creation. Cities are human-built. Nature isn't. I felt a divine presence around me every day."

"In your book Studying With Miss Bishop, you wrote, 'The professions we enter change the way we look at the world and ourselves.' Would you say the same thing about where we live? Did your move from New York to the countryside near Santa Rosa have an immediate impact on your spirit and your outlook?"

"It had an immediate impact as I made the great practical adjustments, but they were often mundane. I had never had to move fallen trees, clear irrigation pipes, or deal with wild boars. There were problems nearly every day. I learned, not very masterfully, lots of practical skills. The more interesting changes happened slowly inside. I began to think of myself as belonging to this place which supposedly belonged to me."

"The Kincade fire must have been devastating."

"The Kincade fire was the largest fire in the history of Sonoma County. It burned 78,000 acres, including twenty of ours. It was the culmination of three years of huge regional wildfires. We had been evacuated twice earlier that year."

"How much of your property was burned?"

"The fire destroyed the homes of most of my neighbors. It burned over my property, but it didn't ignite the structures because I had been scrupulous about clearing brush and trimming trees. But it did great damage. The exterior walls were scorched; all my fences, power lines, irrigation lines, and septic system were destroyed. We had to peel the exterior walls off and rebuild them. It took nearly two years to repair the damage. We were initially told that our house and my studio had been entirely destroyed, so even the mess we found felt like a gift."

"What damage did the fire do to the local landscape?"

"It left the area desolate and black. None of the ground vegetation survived. The ground was covered by ash. The air stank for weeks. The wildlife fled or died. We lost hundreds of trees, including most of the huge old oaks. The hillsides went from heavily wooded to lightly wooded. The flat areas went from woods to meadows. It took three years to clear the burnt trees with injured trees constantly toppling over. We saved some old giants by irrigating their roots and pruning their branches. I also planted two dozen new oaks."

"What a traumatic experience."

"While the fire was traumatic, I must confess that one of the great experiences of my life was to watch the landscape heal itself slowly over the next few years. The madrones grew back from the blackened roots. Thousands of shoots emerged on the same day—Holy Saturday, actually."

Surprised, I say, "On Holy Saturday. That's remarkable."

"The new buckeye shoots came up a few months later. This year, more than four years since the fire, oak shoots appeared on all the hillsides. The birds returned, one species at a time. The repopulation continues. Last night I saw two huge black stag beetles walking on my porch for the first time since the fire. Last week I noted, with less pleasure, that the rattlesnakes had also returned."

"I hate snakes. What about the deer?"

"My pet deer, Betty, came back. I'd known her since she was a fawn. She comes when I call. I feed her our stale bread and vegetables. I was afraid she had died in the fire, but a year later she just showed up."

"You have said that the artist who is most local is often the one who most appeals to a broad audience. How did the move impact your writing? I'm thinking in terms of the impact on your heart's predispositions."

"Much of my early poetry reflected a person who was a wanderer," he replies. "I came from California, but my life led me to other places. I never lost my deep connection to my birthplace. I saw everywhere else, even places I liked, as an outsider. I spent twenty years in the East. Finally, I came home."

"It seems to me," I suggest, "that rootlessness is a common malady for writers."

"So much of American poetry is rootless because the lives of our writers are nomadic," he says. "They are born somewhere and grow up somewhere else. Then they go off to school and move again for graduate school. They take a job in yet another city and continue moving for their career. They don't belong to any specific place. They have a professional perspective on the world—sophisticated but unspecific. In corporate life, I saw the same thing among salespeople who moved from state to state every time they got a promotion."

"How does a life rooted in one locality affect your writing?"

"The world looks different from different places. It helps to know where you stand and see things. I rooted myself in the hills of Sonoma Valley. My daily life does not resemble the worlds of my years in New York and Washington. My days are mostly solitary. None of the people I see regularly went to college. Most of them were born in Mexico. This is just like my early life. My mother was Mexican-American, and we lived in a Mexican neighborhood."

"It changes how you live day-to-day."

"My daily life is a weird combination of physical and intellectual work. I spend part of each day reading and writing. The rest I spend doing manual labor. The chores get harder as I get older. The writing is easier, though the older I get the more difficult it is to convince myself to sit down and get started."

"How did your new home influence your thinking?"

"The most important thing that living in nature taught me was how small and insignificant I am in the scheme of things. I am a momentary observer in the vast and endless unfolding of the world. Having spent my life in huge cities—in major universities, corporations, and public institutions—I had developed a delusional sense of my own importance. That subjectivity was slowly eroded by witnessing the objective reality of the world. Wisdom seemed to know my small piece of the natural world as well as I could. And to love and protect it. I didn't need to think about God when I could feel him everywhere around me."

"A little bit ago, you said, 'Knowing the names of plants changed my relationship to the landscape and the seasons.' How does knowing something's name change how you relate to it?"

"Being able to name a thing means you recognize its individuality," he replies. "You can differentiate it from everything around it."

"Help me understand what you mean."

"Think of it in human terms. If you can't remember a person's name, he or she blurs into the crowd."

"We named our ten acres Brightwing," I say, "from the end of one of my favorite poems, 'God's Grandeur' by Gerard Manley Hopkins. I wanted the name to incite hope in me as I age. Have you thought about naming your property?"

"Many people have suggested we name our hilltop. When we bought it thirty years ago, the poet Donald Justice urged me to name it. That seemed to me a very

Southern thing to do. Naming a homestead allows you to imbue it with your hopes and aspirations. But it also puts a name between you and the thing itself. I like living in a place I can't put a title to."

"In your poem 'Marriage of Many Years,' you say to your wife, Mary, 'You are a language I have learned by heart.' In a different way, wouldn't you say that your land—the trees and the plants, even the rolling hills—has become a language you have learned by heart?"

"Your question answers itself. I spend hours every day outside. I know the property—there is no other word for it—intimately. There are a few places that are too steep for me to visit. Otherwise I know every tree and bush. I can tell you the history of every tree. I've planted them or pruned them. I can tell you when each wildflower blooms and each kind of weed appears."

"Your surroundings have changed, but so has your social life."

"My social life consists mostly of animals and plants. They are good company. I've never been happier."

"Many people are looking for significance. You seem to have found it counterintuitively by realizing how temporary and small you are in the scope of God's work. Is that how you see it?"

"I was a self-directed and disciplined young man. I

had long-term goals and worked steadily toward them. I had the delusion that I could control my own destiny. I led my life guided by a laser. I needed to discover a lamp—a way of seeing everything around me, not just my narrow path."

Recognizing myself, I say, "Being driven seems easier to me than learning to see myself within a larger context. That mindset requires humility."

"Yes, it does. Thomas Aquinas once defined humility as seeing things as they really are. Living here has taught me humility."

"Aldo Leopold, in his book The Sand County Almanac, has an interesting line. I wonder if you have found it to be true. He writes, "Every farm woodland, in addition to yielding lumber, fuel, and posts, should provide its owner a liberal education. This crop of wisdom never fails, but it is not always harvested."

"I work outside every day. I can't do as much as I used to, but I still spend a few hours, some in the morning, some in late afternoon, doing chores. It is routine work—clearing brush, pruning trees, irrigating plants, repairing stone walls. I do the same things over and over. It never bores me. I always see something new. I learn something unexpected."

"To some people, that sounds idyllic."

"I fear I sound like a drippy character from a Jean-Jacques Rousseau novel, an innocent child of nature. That couldn't be less true. I am an intellectual. I spend most of my time reading, thinking, writing. That is why this second life is so important to me. Today I spent a few hours writing about Hugo von Hofmannsthal's Die Frau ohne Schatten (The Woman without a Shadow); and then I dragged huge piles of cut brush down the hill. Immersion in the physical world has saved my poetry from becoming disembodied and abstract."

"You've dedicated your life to cultivating this property. What are the similarities between cultivating your land and cultivating culture through writing?"

"Let's not overstate the quality of my labor. I've spent thirty years mucking around in all sorts of weather to preserve the natural beauty and vitality of this place. I'll win no blue ribbon at the county fair. I do what I can. I am now in my early seventies. But the trees, native plants, and wildlife are thriving. Literary life is also an ecosystem. Each part depends on the others. Without good schools, we don't have capable readers. Without educated readers, good writing won't be recognized. Without strong critics, writers exist in a vacuum. Without strong editors and publishers, authors can't find their public."

"When you look back over your life, are you pleased with the cultural cultivation you were able to accomplish?"

"I gave seven years of my creative life to public service at the National Endowment for the Arts. I was able to create several significant literary programs such as Poetry Out Loud, the national high school poetry recitation competition. Five million teenagers have memorized and recited in those annual contests. The program had a measurable impact. Over the next decade, readership of poetry doubled among teenagers and young adults."

"Your property is a beautiful and hospitable space," I say. "You've worked hard to tend and steward it. Do you see your writing similarly—as an act of hospitality, an opportunity to build something that will be welcome and refresh your readers?"

"I believe that literature is a conversation. The writer needs to engage the reader in an open and intimate dialogue. The author's voice is public; readers respond in the privacy of their minds and imagination. There are many kinds of conversations since human experience is various. The vitality of the conversation is the true measure of an author. Great authors sustain a lively exchange across centuries."

"What would you advise for writers who want to cultivate culture and make a difference in the world?"

"Never lie or condescend to your readers. Treat them as equals, even if you might disagree with them on many things. Believe that there always exists some common ground in our common humanity. That sounds obvious, but there is factionalism, even hate, in the literary world today. There is also too much genteel and self-serving dishonesty. Friedrich Nietzsche said, 'The poets, the poets lie too much.' That is truer than ever. It is so easy to strike an impressive posture. It takes courage and intelligence to speak truth. Someone will be offended."

"Does this lack of honesty and candor, this disrespect for the reader, relate to a sense of place?"

"Oddly, yes. Ansel Adams said, 'A good photograph is knowing where to stand.' Most people today don't know exactly where they stand. Their lives are uncentered. They look around and try to stand like everyone else. It seems the sensible thing to do—to merge into a crowd. (Nowadays it isn't even a real crowd, just a virtual one.) That is why a sense of place is important. You need to speak truthfully from your own experience. You can never fully know the truth, but you do know when you're lying or obfuscating. You approach the truth by refusing to lie. Being fully present in a place allows you to see a few things, however small and local, accurately. It gives you a better ability to judge the larger claims you hear."

"So what exactly is your place?"

"I am a working-class, Latin, West-Coast Catholic. Writing is my trade. It's portable, but I do it best on native soil. I love my place and my people. Despite a few tragedies, I've been lucky in life. My deepest loyalties remain with the world of my childhood—the working poor, especially immigrants. There is dignity in work and honor in doing something well. My uncle Giacomo was a master carpenter and cabinetmaker. Every joint and surface he made was perfect. Fifty years later, his work is still sturdy and handsome. That's my goal as a writer."

California Hills in August
by Dana Gioia

I can imagine someone who found
these fields unbearable, who climbed
the hillside in the heat, cursing the dust,
cracking the brittle weeds underfoot,
wishing a few more trees for shade.

An Easterner especially, who would scorn
the meagerness of summer, the dry
twisted shapes of black elm,
scrub oak, and chaparral, a landscape
August has already drained of green.

One who would hurry over the clinging
thistle, foxtail, golden poppy,
knowing everything was just a weed,
unable to conceive that these trees
and sparse brown bushes were alive.

And hate the bright stillness of the noon
without wind, without motion,
the only other living thing
a hawk, hungry for prey, suspended
in the blinding, sunlit blue.

And yet how gentle it seems to someone
raised in a landscape short of rain—
the skyline of a hill broken by no more
trees than one can count, the grass,
the empty sky, the wish for water.

MALCOLM GUITE

"One of the things I consciously resist and rebel against is the idea of poetry as just personal self-expression. The idea of the lonely, romantic genius in his weird, peculiar place whom everyone has to make allowances for leads to this kind of confessional poetry which gets worse and worse and more and more obscure. What does it amount to? Another strange adventure in the little world of me. I don't buy that at all. No, I want to be the bard of a tribe, to tell the great, collective stories that bind us together—but, of course, I tell them as they've happened to me."

—*Malcolm Guite*

Many years ago, one of my daughters went through a difficult season. Walking with a child through the valley of the shadow of death is a daunting journey that accentuates one's dependence on God; at least, it did so for me. Feeling my limitations rather acutely one day, I decided to take her on an overnight camping trip to the Saint Joe River. I had two modest goals for the trip: first, to enjoy the mountain air and what Wendell Berry called "the peace of wild things," and, second, to memorize Malcolm Guite's 'Singing Bowl.'

That's why, to begin our conversation, I thank Malcolm for the poem and for giving me the words I needed when I needed them, words that could minister to my daughter when my own words had run their course.

As he lights his pipe, he says, "Well, you know, at the time I wrote that poem, I thought I was writing a poem about how to write poetry, but it turned out to be a poem about prayer and living a life open to God. It was a bit of a revelation to me, because I was feeling a bit of a tug between my vocation as a priest and my vocation as a poet. I was wondering if I was sort of robbing Peter to pay Paul. One of the effects of that poem was to help me realize that, no, these are really two sides of the same coin."

"What is your most popular poem?"

"Well, let's see. It's probably 'My Poetry Is Jamming Your Machine.' Of course, if I'm measuring strictly on grateful correspondence, I get quite a bit of responses to a couple of poems I wrote about darkness, difficulty, and depression. The first one is 'The Third Fall' and the other is 'The Christian Plummet.' People from all walks of life share how the poem touched them in particular ways that surprise me, you know. One of the things about poetry is that it's always about more than you think it's about. That's almost my definition of a poem. I usually have some idea of what I'm going to write about, but if I write it down and it turns out to be exactly what I set out to write about and nothing more, then I don't think it's a poem—it's a note to self. It has to quicken itself in the making and push back against me a little and take some sort of living form. It has to resist me a bit in order for me to know that it's a poem."

"You bring up depression. Many of your poems are helpful companions during dark times. When your poems touch on difficulty, they do so as one who has experienced it, and yet you're such a jolly man. How is that?"

"Ah, yes, well, a couple of things about that." He laughs. "As you know, these are things we all share in common. One of the things I consciously resist and rebel against is the idea of poetry as just personal self-expression. The idea of the lonely, romantic genius in his weird, peculiar place whom everyone has to make allowances for leads to this kind of confessional poetry which gets worse and worse and more and more obscure. What does it amount to? Another strange adventure in the little world of me. I don't buy that at all. No, I want to be the bard of a tribe, to tell the great, collective stories that bind us together—but, of course, I tell them as they've happened to *me*. Whatever is personal of mine is most emphatically not in the poems as purely self-expression. Confessional poetry becomes very tedious after a while. The poetry I want to write and that I enjoy reading articulates the joys and sorrows of life. As to the jollity, I suppose I would say that anyone with lighter emotions who hasn't experienced any pain is in danger of sentimentality. I trust them about as much as I trust a Thomas Kinkade painting. You know, there's a term J. R. R. Tolkien coined: 'eucatastrophe.' *Eu* means good, so it's a good catastrophe—but a catastrophe still means catastrophe. In some sense, the eucatastrophe at the end of *The Lord of the Rings* is trustworthy because we've been with these characters to the very edge of the crack of doom. That's why I trust the resurrection, because the church doesn't backpedal on Good Friday."

"While we're on the topic, who called depression 'the black dog'? Was that Winston Churchill?"

"Churchill used it, but it comes from Samuel Johnson who was, as you know, a great Christian, but he had terrible periods of darkness. He was doggedly latched onto Christianity, though. It's a very helpful metaphor, because a dog is both a domestic thing as well as a potentially dangerous thing. In my own life, there have been times when depression was quite severe."

"I'm glad I'm not alone," I say.

"Here's something interesting," he says. "I've always been an enthusiast for sailing. Someone once asked me what floats my boat and I said, 'Well, it's quite literally floating on a boat.' I remember ardently reading a book about cruising around on small boats and the chapter on seasickness. It had pages upon pages of apparently useful information, at the end of which it said most of this would probably not work. But the last words of the chapter were, 'In the end, the best you can do is keep your face into the wind and endeavor to remember that it can't last forever.' I thought that was brilliant and I've applied it to the black dog of depression. I particularly like the phrase 'endeavor to remember' because, obviously, when you are actually feeling seasick, you cannot imagine anything except nausea. It's a totalizing experience. But you can endeavor to remember. You can try to want to remember. One of the best cures for my dark seasons is turning my face to the wind."

"Endeavoring to hope means, I suppose, learning to hope."

"Yes, well, you know, hope is a kind of gift of the Spirit. Hope has one foot in heaven already. It's about the in-breaking of heaven into time. It's not about believing that nothing bad is ever going to happen."

"Your comments have brought something to mind. This question might seem out of the blue, but I promise I'm going somewhere with it. Is Malcolm actually your first name?"

"Ah, I see where you're going with this. No, Malcolm is actually my middle name. My first name is

Ayodeji (*eye-oh-day-jee*). It's a tribal name from Nigeria. Ayo means joy and deji means again, so a double joy. I was born in Nigeria in 1957, but I was very nearly not born. Due to some complications at my birth, things came to a kind of crisis. I was getting strangled by my umbilical cord. It was nearly the end for my mother and for me, before I had even seen the light of day. Anyway, there was only one person who was able to make the necessary interventions and he was just leaving the compound in his car. A nurse ran out and stopped him and he performed a fairly swift Cesarean section, which saved both my mother and me. My mother, being obviously very grateful to the nurse, asked her what to name me and the nurse said Ayodeji, because it is a traditional name for a second child—which I am—and because it was very nearly sorrow rather than joy, but joy was granted, which makes it a double joy."

"That's an incredible story."

"Yes, it is. G. K. Chesterton said that there are people who will point to a man who had great promise in life but who was a failure in the end, and say, 'That man is a Great Might-Have-Been.' Chesterton resists this phrase. He believes everything hangs by so thin a thread that every one of us is a 'Great Might-Not-Have-Been.' The fact that we exist at all is a cause for great rejoicing. It's so helpful to think of one's life as an unexpected bonus rather than a deserved certainty."

"That perspective would change how we enter each day. I'm amazed that you have so thoroughly lived into your name's meaning. That probably happens to people a lot more than we realize. Do you agree?"

"Yes, absolutely. You know, my middle name, Malcolm, has become more and more significant to me. It was chosen by my grandmother. The first meaning of my name is I'm a disciple of Saint Columba who evangelized Scotland, which, in terms of Celtic Christianity, suits me just fine. But its deeper meaning is that I'm a servant of the Spirit. That leaves us with my last name which is rather inexplicable. My father's family came over probably from the south of France, with the Huguenots after the Edict of Nantes. I can find no meaning for it except for a Provençal dialect word that means 'madman.' So I think that fits fairly well."

We're both laughing so hard that it takes me a moment to collect my wits. Finally, I say, "Talking to you reminds me of a quote from the book, *One Long River of Song*. Brian Doyle writes, 'I walked out so full of hope I'm sure I spilled some at the door.' That's you in a nutshell. Your mother couldn't have known that

that was the little boy she was bringing into the world, but it seems to me that it's what you continually do."

"Well, everything comes and goes, but I am, essentially, hopeful because of the great saying of Jesus from the cross: 'It is finished.' A corner has been turned. Darkness has been defeated. Because people like a rehearsed testimony, they ask if I know on what day I was saved and I say, 'Yes, it was Good Friday, same as you.'"

"Amen, brother."

"I think we're entitled to joy—a real joy, not a naive optimism," he says. "Václav Havel writes somewhere that hope is not the certainty that things will turn out well, but that they will make sense—that they will mean something."

"Okay," I say, "I'm going to yank the steering wheel and veer off of this road and onto a new one."

"Yes, fine, fine."

"What's your take on the fact that the reincarnation of Bilbo Baggins—if I may call you that—has nearly 100,000 followers on YouTube?"

He laughs and ruffles his hair. "I'm just being me. There's nothing more than that. It began, more or less, during the first couple of days of the COVID-19 lockdown in 2020. I was still engaged at Cambridge as chaplain as well as teacher, but I was stuck in my little village and my students were stuck wherever they were and none of us could meet. My entire mode of being chaplain was about presence and about being glad to welcome people. Insofar as I had a spiritual discipline, it was a ministry of presence. My golden rule, the thing I prayed to be given, was to be glad to be interrupted. Whatever I was doing, when someone knocked on my door, even if I was right in the middle of a particularly delicate sentence, I would remind myself that this is a good thing and I would say, 'Come, come in.' That's how I start every video. So that little video thing was my way of pretending that we could still meet, you see. It was meant only for my students and a handful of friends. I suppose I've become a bit of what they call an influencer, but I would have been voted boy most unlikely to become one." He chuckles. "I find it amusing that people who take YouTube seriously, who work really hard at it and have fewer followers, are writing to ask about my strategies, about all this technical stuff—lighting, schedule, staging, and all the rest—God help us all! People," he shouts, "there is no strategy!"

"So why the following?"

"I think social media and YouTube have become such contested, nauseating, and poisonous places that what I offer is something a very large number of people need—this quiet little haven and a feeling that some sense of truth, beauty, and simplicity has been restored to them. Honestly, my hope is that my videos will help people stop watching YouTube altogether and go read a book. That's the whole game of it. What we're happily accepting is the illusion that there are no screens involved in this encounter at all."

"And you're just delighting in what you enjoy—namely, good books. It's hospitality and boyish enthusiasm."

"Yes, exactly."

"When I spoke to the poet James Matthew Wilson, he described a crisis he faced during his post-grad work. The very thing that drew him to study the humanities—the love of good writing and of good stories—was replaced by deconstruction and political theory."

"It's really true. I'm glad I got out of academia before all of that really took off. It won't last. I mean, theory tends to eat itself in the end. All of the structuralism, post-structuralism, and critical deconstruction has already begun to deconstruct itself. People have started returning to reading with the grain of the text rather than against the grain."

"That's what you're doing on your YouTube channel, and it's refreshing."

"I hope so," he replies.

"Samuel Taylor Coleridge has been a major influence on your life. When did you first encounter his work?"

"Coleridge is huge. You know, if you read at all widely, you're bound to find writers who feel like kindred spirits with whom you resonate. Coleridge is very much that for me. I empathize with him enormously. I met his poetry first because my mother had a huge fund of poetry memorized by heart from which she would pull as the occasion arose. When I was a kid, we spent a great deal of time traveling by sea, you know. Returning to England from Nigeria every year took quite a long time back in those days. It was always quite a moment when the ship would leave the harbor and we would watch the furrow and the wake of the boat. And she would quote 'The Rime of the Ancient Mariner,' saying, 'We were the first to burst into that silent sea.' And, of course, I would want to hear more. So I knew that poem quite well. I started diving into his work more seriously later in high school, reading his prose and so on. I found him very interesting."

He gazes out the window for a moment, takes a puff from his pipe, and then continues.

"When I began to make the intellectual and imaginative journey back into Christianity, having rejected it in my teens, I had this memory that Coleridge had quite a bit to say about this. So I went back to him and found that he had written this wonderful, mature, and philosophically deeply grounded return to a fully Trinitarian faith. I looked again at the textbooks we've been given about Coleridge, and there's nothing at all about that. They just portray him as this romantic ruin, as it were. There's a lot about opium, but almost nothing about God. Secular historians tend to airbrush out what they're not interested in, to see religious faith as a kind of background noise to action. So I resolved that, one day, I would write an account of Coleridge that restored the full picture. That book became *Mariner*, in which I set out to make a case for his relevance and our need for him in the cultural crisis we enter today. I found in him a companion, especially when it came to his view of the imagination as a truth-bearing faculty."

"Coleridge has been more than a companion—he has strengthened your foundations."

"Yes, and now I find him at my side again. One of my childhood dreams was to write an Arthuriad, as it's called. I was searching for the poetic form and found it in the ballad form, which Coleridge remade, making it capable of carrying great weight. He kept all of the ballad form's lucidity and readability, but he also allowed it to become a vehicle for something beautiful and luminous and permanent. I'm not saying that I'm going to achieve that, you know, but at least I can try."

"How ambitious is this project?"

"If I live long enough to complete the whole thing, it will be four volumes, each volume consisting of three books so that it becomes a proper twelve-book epic."

"So something modest in length, as in the tradition of Virgil and John Milton?"

He laughs. "The whole idea is a little outrageous, I know. It's not, as Jonathan Swift would say, a modest proposal, but, you know, I'm working on it."

"I love it. You've given yourself a project that gets you up in the morning with an eager step."

"Absolutely. The imagination is like any other faculty; you have to exercise it. I'm daunted by the project, of course, but I'm also excited by it. I don't know which day will be my last, but I can only do the work in front of me. I'm in the hands of God. As someone says in Narnia, we're always between the lion's paws, you know. In the end, I just hope that whatever God allows me to complete will be of some good in the world. I want to write something that satisfies every age. George MacDonald said he wanted to write fairy tales for everyone who loves them, from five to fifty-five. I don't want to simply preach to the choir, as it were. What I really want is for some future C. S. Lewis, a brooding atheist teenager, to pick up my Arthur poems and love them just for themselves. And then for him to find that they have given him something with which or through which to discover the truth in Christianity. I want my poems to have snuck past the watchful dragons of our secularism and the immanent frame and actually open something up inside him."

"That's a wonderfully rare vision for one's work. It's so wonderful to imagine that you made me forget my next question."

He ruffles his hair and grins. "I apologize."

"Thinking about C. S. Lewis as a brooding teenager," I say, "reminds me that he said his imagination was baptized. An interesting way of looking at it. MacDonald's work did the heavy lifting, of course, but his walks with Tolkien helped as well."

"Indeed," he says.

"We bought some acreage a few years ago that we hope to build a house on someday. The first thing we did was cut a footpath which we called Addison's Walk, based on the path that Lewis and Tolkien walked in Oxford. People often ask, 'Who is Addison?', so we get to tell them the story."

"Very good. And of course they ought to ask, 'Who is Addison?' Joseph Addison was an English poet and essayist who wrote a brilliant essay in the early 1700s on gratitude and the need to restore the sense of gratitude. In the course of that essay, he presents a poem that has become a great hymn of the Christian church. It begins like this: 'When all thy mercies, O my God, my rising soul surveys, transported with the view, I'm lost in wonder, love, and praise.' Now, that wouldn't be a bad verse to put up on your Addison's Walk."

"Not bad at all. That's a great idea," I say. "It's a fitting verse for your work, too."

"Well, you know, Maggie and I chose that as the opening hymn to our wedding and I timed it so that when I turned to see the bride, I was singing with everyone else, 'Transported with the view, I'm lost in wonder, love, and praise.'"

"That's absolutely beautiful. How long have you two been married?"

"We're going on forty years of marriage."

"What a gift."

"Yes, she has been a gift. You know, she kind of holds the kite strings."

"Maybe we could close this conversation with a poem from your book *Sounding The Seasons*. One of the things I love about your poetry is the sense of a blessing that comes at the close of the poem. Many of your poems resolve in a kind of grace. I was hoping you would read 'Jesus Weeps,' because I think it's fitting for our time—which is to say, I think it's fitting for any time."

"I'd be happy to read it."

Jesus comes near and he beholds the city
And looks on us with tears in his eyes,
And wells of mercy, streams of love and pity
Flow from the fountain whence all things arise.
He loved us into life and longs to gather
And meet with his beloved face to face
How often has he called, a careful mother,
And wept for our refusals of his grace,
Wept for a world that, weary with its weeping,
Benumbed and stumbling, turns the other way,
Fatigued compassion is already sleeping
Whilst her worst nightmares stalk the light of day.
But we might waken yet, and face those fears,
If we could see ourselves through Jesus' tears.

"I guess I was playing with two ideas in that poem," he says. "I wanted to challenge the idea that people are blinded by tears. Since tears are a sign of love, maybe they actually clarify our vision. To know that you've been wept for is to know that you've been loved. The other thing I was trying to wake us up from was compassion fatigue. Is that a phrase used in America?"

"Yes. It's a very real concern, especially for teachers and those in the medical field."

"Yes, well, I played with the idea that if compassion—already so weary—falls asleep, then we're in a really bad spot, totally incapable of response while our worst nightmares parade around. So what is the solution to the problem of compassion fatigue? It seems to me that if we weep with Jesus, if we see ourselves and the world through his tears, then we start seeing people through the compassion of Jesus. We might awaken yet, you know. Jesus renews in us the capacity for compassion, but also the capacity for tears. I think about the great phrase in Virgil's Aeneid, 'lacrimae rerum,' the very tears of things. The fallen world itself is worthy of tears and an elegy. I mean, if the answer to that cliché question 'What would Jesus do?' is to cry, then you should cry."

"And, as you so often remind us, if Jesus were to laugh in a given moment, then we should laugh as well."

"Yes, indeed."

Maundy Thursday Lockdown
by Malcolm Guite

Maundy Thursday, all the world is still
The planes wait, grounded by departure gates
The street is empty and the shopping mall
Deserted. Padlocked, the playground waits
Against the day that children play again
Till then our sad refrain is just refrain.

Maundy Thursday, all the world is still
And Jesus is at supper with his friends
No longer in the upper room, that hall
In Zion where the story starts and ends,
For he descended from it long ago
To find his new friends in the here and now.

Maundy Thursday, all the world is still
And Jesus is at supper with his friends
Our doors are locked for fear, but he has skill
In breaking barriers. With ease he bends
Our prison bars, slips past the sentry post
And joins us as the guest who is our host.

Maundy Thursday All the world is still
But in cramped quarters on the fifteenth floor,
In lonely towers made of glass and steel,
And in the fierce favelas of the poor,
Touching with wounded hands the wounds he tends
Christ Jesus is at supper with his friends.

KAREN
AN-ĦWEI LEE

"Part of me was worried about *kronos* time—carving out enough chronological time to sit at my desk and wait for the writing angel to arrive with inspiration—but God was providing *kairos* time, the opportune moments that are pregnant with God's purpose."

—Karen An-hwei Lee

Karen Lee's office sits on the second floor of Blanchard Hall, a beautiful sandstone building on Wheaton College's campus. It was built in 1853 by Christian abolitionists, and according to a sign by the front entrance, served as a stop on the Underground Railroad. The stone stairs are worn smooth, proof of a long history. She welcomes me joyfully and offers caramel popcorn, a treat I eagerly accept. Through one large window I can see the grounds. A basket of foil-wrapped chocolates sits on her desk with a sign that says, "Gratitude Basket." Books surround us. Several books sit on the table, including Luci Shaw's latest, *Reversing Entropy*.

"I'm so glad you have Luci Shaw's newest book," I say. "It's hard to believe that in her mid-nineties, she's still writing for publication."

"Her longevity and creative productivity are inspiring."

"The title is provocative," I say. "I feel like I'm raising my children in a time of widespread entropy."

"You're not alone," she replies. "The last few years have had a dramatic impact on us."

"How has the societal upheaval impacted you?"

"I joined Wheaton during the pandemic," she says. "There was so much change and uncertainty throughout the world at the time."

"I assume you had to suspend writing just to do your administrative work."

"Actually, poetry brought about immediacy and human connection in a time of distancing. Faculty invited me to share devotionals with their departments or with groups of students remotely. I decided to write poems of hope and to share them during those devotionals. People need poetry during times of crisis. Part of me was worried about *kronos* time—carving out enough chronological time to sit at my desk and wait for the writing angel to arrive with inspiration—but God was providing *kairos* time, the opportune moments that are pregnant with God's purpose. I believe that God used these little poems to serve as ambassadors of hope in the midst of a challenging season."

"I bet you didn't see that coming when you took the job."

"Not at all. In fact, I offered my writing to God as a sacrifice beforehand because I understood that the administrative load would be heavy. In prayer, I told the Lord, 'I love writing, but if you want to take it from me, then I offer it freely. I know that I am your *poiema*. That is enough. I will let my life be the poem."

"That's a hard but necessary prayer," I say, "especially if poetry had been part of your life from a young age."

"Yes. I think I fell in love with poetry early in life. I had a first-grade teacher who made little chapbooks with us. We would place small plants, drawings, and descriptions in these books. She would hold each one up and read it to the class. Her delight made us feel important. I remember one of these chapbooks had a cardboard cover, saddle-stitched with yarn, and there was a picture of my face on the cover. I remember feeling like I was an author and showing it to my classmates, who had their own chapbooks just like mine."

"We need more teachers like her. Why do you write? Is it to explore life? Or a way of talking to yourself? What compels you to write poems?"

"It depends on the season of life," she says. "For a long time, it was a way of processing my experiences. Like everyone else, I'm affected by what's going on around me. Poetry became a way of coming to terms with those things, of exploring my emotions, of discovering what I truly thought about a situation or an idea."

"Your poetry leans toward the abstract."

"Yes, one book reviewer said, over a decade ago, that I risk the inaccessible. It was a kind way of saying that my poetry can be a little abstruse—in a daring way. Some readers find my poems not denotative enough and too elliptical. I don't quibble with that. I have always been interested in abstract ideas, in theology and philosophy, as well as nature and life experienced through our senses. I enjoy climbing into those lofty heights out of valleys by way of poetry. But when I was writing for a direct audience during a time of crisis, I couldn't just brew ideas in my own head and write something for myself—or an ideal reader out there. I had to write for people who were walking a shared journey of uncertainty, loss, and grief. There was a communal aspect to my writing and the poems became a little more like offerings."

"Do you feel like those were better poems as a result?"

"It's hard to say," she says. "I like so many kinds of poetry. There are different modes or registers for writing poetry and they're all valuable. They may not all be universally appreciated, but they're still valuable forms of expression."

"The poet Geoffrey Hill wrote, "To love, determinedly and well, and to be / unfaithful: there should have arisen / particular broken forms to engage this." Does poetry provide these broken forms? What makes broken forms the most effective way to engage our relational and societal disintegration?"

"The fracturing of the human consciousness and our lived experience is all around us, but poetry can help us kneel among the fragments—yes, even anneal them. The Japanese art of *kintsugi* is a wonderful expression of this kind of healing. An artist takes broken vessels and glues them together, but instead of hiding the cracks, she highlights the jagged breaks with gold paint. This artistic act raises the ordinary, humdrum object to something transcendent and beautiful. In a similar way, the broken yet fluid form of free verse—with its irregular margins and fragmentary utterances—can raise our broken experience to something extraordinary. Because they're broken, poems can bleed light."

"What do you mean?"

"I'm not sure how else to say it. Poetry is a shared experience, even a form of communion, insofar as it is an exchange of intimate thoughts or emotions. As a poet, I believe that words matter, but maybe there is a dimension that draws us closer to the musical realm where language is a form of embodied experience. Instead of striving to find precise meanings or representation all the time, maybe we should let the words float over us, let them bring us to a place of contemplation."

"You're calling us to experience poetry as a form of meaning-making that is not transactional. I shouldn't approach poetry like I approach an essay."

"That's correct. Even if a poem eludes meaning upon a first reading, upon further reading or upon further contemplation it might open onto new revelations. That's true of the human heart as well. From the *pathos* of emotions to the *benthos*—the bottom of the sea—there is so much unknown to explore."

"Who are the poets that are your example in this exploration of the human experience?"

"Emily Dickinson is at the top of that list. Sometimes her poems are difficult to understand, but she never shies away from engaging what is happening in her heart—or even in her brain. In a society of distraction and anxiety, her poems bring us back to authentic human connection, spiritually and corporeally, as well as metaphysical questions."

"The Wheaton motto is *For Christ and His Kingdom.* Do you share that vision for your poetry?"

"In this season, my poems serve my immediate community, which makes my writing an act of worship. I often think in terms of cultural and spiritual work when it comes to writing poems. If this poem travels very far, will it be strong enough to do the spiritual work necessary to build Christ's kingdom, even if just a little? It becomes a humble offering, a way to bear Christ's message of hope."

"So much of that ministry is out of your control. Once your poems are in the world, they take on a life of their own."

"That often happens. The poems grow legs like grasshoppers and do wonderful things I wouldn't have ever imagined."

"Colossians says Christ is before all things and holds all things together. The book of Acts says that in Christ we live and move and have our being. You strike me as a poet who is leaning hard into those revelations, into the mystery of God and into the mystery that is the self."

"I hope so. I think I'm trying to investigate or discern the complexities of the Creator's weaving that holds all things together, to discover more about myself and more about the one who made me. Without Christ, I think my poems just fall apart. Like me, my poems find their meaning, their resolution, and their inspiration in Christ. When I'm truly awake to the presence of the divine in the ordinary, my poems point back to Christ like mini-compasses."

"In your poem 'Songs of Comfort,' you write, 'God is waiting for us to pay attention.' What is the poet's role in helping us pay attention? Would you say that poets are God's emissaries to help us wake up?"

"I love that idea. Yes, I think poets are God's emissaries. Poetry is a vehicle for attention; it can create the space in us that makes revelation possible. There are so many ways in which we can pay attention—the mind, the heart, the imagination. We're familiar with *lectio divina*, a method of praying with Scripture or "divine reading," but there's also *visio divina* as a way of praying with the eyes or "divine seeing." Writing poetry helps me pay attention to what's going on around me and inside me. Reading poetry can help me do that, too."

"Some people listen in *kronos* time and some listen in *kairos* time. Would you say that the best poets seem to listen in *kairos* time, that they're listening to a higher register?"

"I think some of my favorite poets have a high antenna."

"Are they born with it?"

"Maybe some of them are, but I think it's really a matter of practice. It's like a spiritual discipline, a kind of mindfulness that can be developed. Solitude is an important part of my poetic practice. I do need solitude so that I can declutter the noise in my head. At the same time, I have a deep appreciation for the importance of community. If a poem is going to speak to readers, it needs to come from a place of shared experience. I wrote a poem about artificial intelligence, for example, because it's been a hot topic among my friends and colleagues—how it impacts content generation, pedagogy, research, and our overall engagement with information."

"Community feeds you and you feed community."

"That's my hope."

"Let's talk about artificial intelligence for a minute. It's a field that is growing incredibly quickly. Do you think it's a threat?"

"I don't fear artificial intelligence. It gives us a great chance to ask critical and evaluative questions, to get better at what we do. I think there are spiritual and existential limitations to artificial intelligence. It only knows what we tell it. So, for example, can AI share the gospel? Well, it can offer the information—the requisite Scripture passages, for instance—but isn't there an element of human connection necessary to bridge the gap? I think so. Can AI lead someone through the sinner's prayer? Technically, yes, but there's something missing."

"We're made in the image of God, which means we're all creative. Does AI threaten that divine attribute in us? Will we end up abdicating creativity to computers that we have trained to do our work for us?" I ask.

"I think that's a real possibility," she says. "In technical professions that require analyzing data for patterns, for example, I can see many possibilities for artificial intelligence. But with work that has a spiritual dimension or an inter-relational nature, we might forget how to think for ourselves or how to create for ourselves. Some poets have been experimenting with AI, collaborating with it. I think that's worth doing as a conceptual form of digital poetics, but concurrently, I would also caution against wholesale outsourcing of human thought."

"Li-Young Lee once said that those who read theology and poetry might have heard of the burning bush, but God calls poets to sit in the burning bush and tell us about their direct encounter. AI can't sit in the burning bush."

"What an amazing way to think about poets and their work," she says. "Yes, that spiritual experience is a threshold I don't think AI can or should cross."

"But it might be able to fake religious experience enough to look like the real thing," I add.

"Yes, but only because we taught it to parrot the experience," she replies.

"I was reading a poet the other day who suggested that, generally speaking, we lack the ability to distinguish between authentic and inauthentic religious experience. He compared it to the Beatles and the Monkeys. They may sound similar to the untrained ear, but the former is authentic while the latter is derivative. The same could be said of the heavenly encounter."

"Yes, like the Platonic simulacrum which is mimetic and a couple times removed from the original. There's something deep inside us that longs for that authentic encounter. I guess what I'm saying is that AI can be a useful tool—even with creativity—but we need to intentionally remind ourselves that it's just a tool. It's not a replacement for human engagement. I'm hopeful that we can do that."

"So, human connection will always need humans."

"Yes."

"Josef Pieper says that 'music, the fine arts, poetry—

anything that festively raises up human existence and thereby constitutes its true riches—all derive their life from a hidden root, and this root is a contemplation which is turned toward God and the world so as to affirm them.' It sounds to me like he is saying that the poet's job is to echo God's words in Genesis 1, to show what is good and to declare *it is good*."

"I'm in total agreement. I'm interested in seeking where God is at work, where God is creating good in a fallen world. Sometimes my poems spring from some harrowing event or the darkness we all experience, but it's through the poem that I'm trying to climb into the light. I find so much to affirm in life."

"You like to take everyday moments and raise them to something transcendent. For example, one of my favorites is in your poem, 'On the Flavor of Awe.' In the poem, you're eating ice cream. You ask, 'What is the flavor of unmerited grace? / Just whisper *hosanna* into a round of divinity / when no one is listening.'"

"What can I say? I love ice cream."

"That makes two of us. Your decision to put a sensual term, *flavor*, to something abstract and theological like *unmerited grace* made me stop and pay attention. I'm not sure I have a question on this, maybe I just want to hear you tell me how those ideas come to you."

"I'm afraid you're going to laugh. I was at an ice cream shop and saw a flavor called Divinity. It made me ask, 'What would divinity taste like?' I decided it must taste like awe. Then my brain started asking other questions. 'What is awe? What does it look like when the divine is tasted in our daily, human experience?' There's a sublime layer to all of our existence, even eating ice cream. That's why I like mingling the concrete and the abstract; it's so interesting."

"Eating ice cream is a delightful experience, but not all of life is delightful. We experience adversity, conflict, and deprivation. How does poetry, or the writing of poetry, help you navigate those seasons of life?"

"One of my favorite places to visit is the Mission San Juan Capistrano, in California. There's an enormous millstone in the garden that was used for crushing olives. Whenever I visit, I put my hands on the stone and pray. I draw strength from this image because sometimes it feels like a stone is passing over me, crushing me over and over. I need to be reminded that without crushing, there can be no oil. When the olives are crushed, you get a messy pomace that doesn't taste good and doesn't look beautiful. But after a while, the golden oil runs. In some respects, I'm just an olive being crushed so that oil—or whatever I write—can serve as a balm and as an anointing."

"That's a hope-filled picture," I say.

"I want to be a hope-filled person, so I draw inspiration from hopeful images."

"It takes a great deal of patience and courage to sit beneath the stone."

"I think you're correct," she says. "We're so focused on self-preservation or on our own agendas, that we often forget what God might be doing for us and through us."

"Jeremiah 33:3 says, 'Call to me and I will answer you and I will tell you great and hidden things that you have not known.' You're trying to stay attuned to the voice of God even in hardship."

"Yes, that's right. It's Psalm 42:7, deep calling unto deep."

Spiritus Mundi: On Artificial Intelligence
by Karen An-hwei Lee

You shadow us, expanding like a data cloud without mist,
neither the largest tree system in the world named Pando,
aspen forest of clones; nor the honey mushroom, a fungus
lacing its invisible hyphae over a couple thousand acres,

older than you and I. In our deepest seas of information,
no distinction exists between my voice and your artfulness,
whispering about a ransom or muttering about gift cards.
Your end-stopped, rhymed doggerel does not say much

about your source texts. I ask you about me—who am I?
What do you know about my memories, my life's purpose
on this pear-shaped planet, where I am a half century old?
Can you tell your hands from mine? Are you tethered

to our sleep? Do you appear in our dreams? How many
     sheep
do you lead back to the flock? You do not know me. In fact,
you say nothing about my avocation. You must be trained,
and I have taught you nothing yet.

LI-YOUNG LEE

"I suppose that every picture Christ enters becomes Christic. It becomes organized around the most spectacular, the greatest Good. That's what matters now. That's the only thing that matters, Ben. All that's left for me is to break the oil over his feet. All that's left are love songs to God."

—*Li-Young Lee*

Many years ago, Li-Young Lee met me in a dream. It was a first for me; no other author had made such a visitation. In the dream, I lived in one of Indonesia's crowded cities. It was after midnight, and the city's neon lights flickered and glowed outside my high-rise apartment window. I heard a knock at the door and opened it to find him standing there, smiling, his long black hair pulled back. I welcomed him in. He sat in my favorite chair while I boiled water for tea.

I couldn't believe my good fortune. Now I could tell him thank you for writing some of my favorite poems. I told him how elated I was to see him. I told him that I first read one of his books while stuck in traffic and it opened my eyes to beauty and joy. Tears welled up in my eyes. I turned my back.

"You must be used to effusive fans," I said.

I heard him reply, "Thank you, that means so much."

While I prepared his tea, I told him about the season in my life when I carried one of his books around with me.

It was a hard time of life for me, but working through his poems, one line at a time, helped.

"I didn't always know what you were saying, but somehow I understood," I told him. "I didn't comprehend in my mind, but I got it in my heart. Does that make sense?"

I turned around. The room was empty, the front door ajar. Still holding the tea cup, I stepped outside hoping to find him, but he was gone. All I had wanted to do was serve him a little tea to say thank you. Now, the tears flowed unhindered. I openly sobbed. "I have your tea," I called into the night, but the city's throbbing drowned out my feeble voice.

That's when I woke up, grief-stricken.

You can understand, then, why it felt dreamlike to see him walking toward me in real life. He wore black, and though it was a sunny day, he carried a brightly colored umbrella. My travel plans had brought me to Chicago, so we decided to meet at a little park near his home. We had exchanged many emails over the previous month—rearranging schedules, considering what we might discuss—and both of us were excited to finally spend a couple of hours together.

He greets me with a wide grin. "You know, like an idiot, I let my expectations for this meeting get too high," he says. "I'm sorry, but there's nowhere to go from here but down."

I laugh. "Well, we might as well enjoy the ride, then. Do you remember the story about Saint Augustine walking the beach? He sees a little boy carrying ocean water in a shell to dump into a little hole he has dug in the sand. Augustine says, 'Hey kid, what are you doing?' The boy replies, 'I'm trying to fit the ocean in this hole.'"

"What a story."

"Isn't that what we are attempting? We're just two kids trying to capture the ocean?"

"I hope so. I really do. I just returned from Toronto, where I witnessed some heavy-duty ocean scooping in a painting. It agitated and troubled me so much that it's all I can think about right now. I'm not even sure I'm capable of conversation; I'm just so distracted."

"Tell me more."

"I visited the Ontario Museum of Art. There's a seventeenth-century painting by Mattia Preti called 'Saint Paul the Hermit.' It unseated me. The painting might be life-size, I don't know. In it, there's so much darkness descending on Paul. So much darkness, Ben. I mean, his robe is falling away from his frail body. At the top, there's a raven's head with a morsel of bread in its beak, and Paul is straining toward that bread. He's straining into that darkness. It's a darkness full of news."

"What kind of news?" I ask.

"I don't know," he replies. "Ultimately, news that's profound and great, news we've forgotten, news we can barely believe. When I saw that painting, I just had to stand beneath it. I thought: 'It is finished.' I don't know why that phrase came to me, but that's all I could think about. *It is finished.* I felt this ecstatic thing, this realization that it really *is* finished. I'm just standing in the wake."

"Those are the words Christ spoke at his darkest point. Is that the darkness you're talking about?"

"I don't know. I'm still wrestling with it. There's a darkness that's pregnant with meaning, you know. It's a different kind of darkness. It's not merely dark; it's something more."

"You're reminding me of that passage in Isaiah 50 where God calls his people to trust in the name of the Lord, even when they walk in darkness. He says that if we encircle ourselves with light of our own making—some kind of artificial and temporary reprieve from the darkness—then we will lie down in torment. Such a profound confrontation can happen, but we're afraid of it. We don't feel strong enough to sit in it, so we distract ourselves."

"Yes, that's the darkness I'm talking about. That's exactly what I'm feeling. It's absolutely uncomfortable. While in Toronto, I attended an art exhibit for a young artist I know personally. I love him deeply. His pieces were so stirring that I can't get them out of my head. They were full of the same darkness I witnessed in the painting by Mattia Preti. A darkness full of yearning, full of good news, but it was so dark. I mean, can you imagine the courage it takes for an artist to enter that darkness with each new project?"

"It would take a great deal of courage and an unusual attentiveness."

"Yes, it was so beautiful. As long as he can do the work, he's going to be okay. Without the art, I don't know. Maybe the work keeps us from losing our minds in the darkness. But I think of that painting by Preti and those words, 'It is finished.' Everything has changed for me. You catch me at a moment of crisis, Ben. I don't know that I can write the poems I've been writing all these years. In fact, I know I can't. I've been writing poems as if I was living *before* it is finished. It's hard to catch up, to awaken to the reality that *it is finished*. I've been lagging behind. What do I write now?"

"What makes your work, even the book you just released, a pre-*it is finished* book?"

"It's as if the book didn't hear the news. None of my previous poems had heard the news. Maybe they heard whispers of it, but only whispers."

The two of us sit together silently. By now, the tiny park has filled with playing children. An errant volleyball rolls toward us, and I toss it back.

"I suppose the news was there," he says, "but my poems lagged behind somehow. That's the thing: the news is Christ. It's all Christ. There's no other name, no other word for it. All of creation is shouting the news. That tree over there is Christic; that fountain is Christic. Every one of us is in the wake of the good news that *it is finished.* The world is changed. No, it's bigger than that, something much bigger. *Everything* has changed. It's all true."

"When Christ said 'It is finished' on the cross, it was, in some way, not the end, but the beginning," I say. "It was a declaration of a new beginning. His work was complete, but the work we do—the post-*it is finished* work—has just begun."

"Yes! What is that work, Ben?"

"Isn't it all praise? Isn't it simply adoration and gratitude in all its forms?"

"Yes, yes! But how? What does that look like for the poet? You know, the paintings I saw were so full of praise—pure, uncensored praise, but it's a praise that's rooted in darkness. And the painting by Mattia Preti was so full of black paint. It's so black under Paul's chin. There's black behind him and beside him, but not the same intensity of black that you would find in an abstract painting. There are so many variations. Each one is important when it comes to depicting the male figure in agony. I was talking to my son about the history of this figure in art: John Milton's 'Samson Agonistes,' the crucified Christ, William Blake's work, all these paintings I saw at the exhibit. I don't know what to call it except maybe the agony of an ecstatic experience or the agony of a revelation."

"It's not the same agony that accompanies those who die without hope," I say.

"What do you mean by that?" he asks.

I consider for a moment. "Maybe not all deaths are equal. The agony of those without hope is not the same as the agony you saw in the painting of Paul. His agony had meaning."

"Yes, that's it. There's meaning in that darkness. Much of life isn't that way, you know. There is so much that lacks meaning. This young painter whom I love, whose work was so magnificently charged with presence, went through a very dark void when he was younger. He had a great job; he was making a large amount of money, but he felt empty. He said, 'None of this means anything. None of this is Christic.' I told him, 'What you see is true. None of it counts.' I feared for him at the time. I mean, how do you deal with that sudden realization of bankruptcy? It's a difficult and dangerous endeavor to live in a world so oppressed by meaninglessness."

"But," I say, "*it is finished*."

"Yes, that's right. I have come to a realization, Ben. It's Christmas every day and the devil all the time. Both are true. That's what that painting of Paul told me. That's the Christic—all the light accounted for, all the polarities accounted for, everything accounted for."

"How do we work that revelation into our poetry?"

"That's the difficult place I find myself in today," he replies. "I'm not sure. I'm trying to work it out. I'm playing with a formula in my head."

"Do you have it worked out enough to share?"

"Maybe, maybe not. What I have so far is quite simple. Poetry, in its essence, is the voice of Being itself divided by a being or Little Being. Like this." He uses his hands to show the division in the air.

Absolute Being, or God

———————————

Little Being, the poet

"Can you help me understand?" I ask.

"I'm not sure," he replies. "Maybe I have it upside down, I don't know. I'm not offering much clarity. I'm not really answering any questions."

"Sounds to me like we're doing exactly what we set out to do," I reply. "We're just trying to capture the ocean."

"That's a relief," he says. And after a moment, "It's also very humbling. Look, Ben, I made a bargain with God, and I need to deliver on that bargain. And when it comes to interviews, I need to cover some things about poetry, and then we can talk about whatever you want."

"Let's do that."

We sit quietly for a moment, watching the games around us, listening to the children shout and squeal.

"I guess what I want to say is that I'm always in the throes of trying to understand the tension between stillness and motion. I sometimes call stillness 'silence,' but people don't understand. They see white space around a poem on the page and call the white space silence, but it's not silent. The white space is full of noise. The craft, the magic, the Christic imagination that uses words to make a reader *feel* silence requires a stillness *in the poet*. Stillness is the mind being still. All language in a chain—one word linked to the next word—is motion.

We study that motion. We notice that it is stressed and unstressed. The great poets see that it consists of weak forces and strong forces. They really boiled things down for us in a way that can be useful, but it's not enough. It's the stillness *inside* the poet that makes the poem. It's the stillness that returns the poet to the source."

"What do you mean?"

"Look, when you read a poem on the page, the line keeps pulling you back to the left margin, to the beginning. There used to be a convention of capitalizing the first letter of each line to tell the reader that we're starting over. I don't like capitalizing the first letter because it feels cluttered to me, noisy. It makes me feel anxious and forget what I'm doing. What am I doing? Robert Frost called it 'the tribute of the current to the source.' Each line is a tribute of the current to the source, to the beginning of the poem."

"He's talking about the poetic line."

"Yes," he says, "but he's also talking about something much bigger than that. He's saying that our motions and words have to pay tribute to the Source."

"What does that look like? How does a poet do that?"

"We do that by ransoming each poetic line with as much meaning as possible—by infusing it with the news we were talking about earlier. You know, the incredible news that I felt in the darkness of those paintings and in the agony of their subjects. All these years, I thought I knew what the news was—that life is beautiful despite everything, or something—and maybe that's still the news, but it's so much more than that, and I'm grappling with what the expression of that news looks like."

The park has gradually filled—more children, more games—and we realize that we have been shouting over the clamor. "We have so much more to explore," he says, "but maybe we can find another place to talk."

I gather my things. He holds his umbrella in one hand and a small paper cup nearly emptied of coffee. We walk along the sidewalk and continue talking.

"I keep coming back to this Christic imagination," he says. "Everything depends on it. Everything exists by virtue of the Christic. Christ was at the very beginning of the world, and everything participates in Christ, whether we know it or not. As a pastor's son, I grew up hearing this news, but it means much more than I ever realized. If people knew it and could remember it, there would be far less suffering, I think."

"Are you hyper-aware of human suffering?"

"Oh my, yes. Absolutely. I live in Chicago. My neighborhood is like a parade of suffering."

The sun breaks out from behind a cloud; its heat is beating down upon us. Li-Young opens his umbrella and lifts it high to shade me as we walk.

"This is a thing we do in China," he says.

Feeling more than a little uncomfortable, like I should be the one holding the umbrella over him, I say, "Thank you. That's very kind."

By now, we've come to another park, a larger one flanked by eight lanes of traffic on Lake Shore Drive, but green grass is welcoming and, aside from a few homeless shelters, relatively empty. We sit down in the shade, clover all around us.

"Going back to your obligation to God," I say, "have you told me everything you need to say about poetry? I don't want to move on until you've said your peace."

"I think so. I guess I just wanted to say all glory be to God. There's no poetry without God. I mean, there's *nothing* without God. That's all I wanted to say."

"In God's timing, I'm meeting you just a couple of days after your encounter with *it is finished*. You called it a crisis, but it is also a kind of revelation."

"Absolutely. I mean, it is a crisis. I have to start over, but I don't know how. That's not easy at my age."

"Does it create anxiety in you? Excitement?"

"Both. I'm terrified."

"One of my favorite books is *The Peregrine*, by J. A. Baker. For about half a year, he tracked the daily activities of a pair of peregrine falcons in England. It's beautifully written. At one point, he says, 'The hunter must become the thing he hunts.' Maybe you need to imitate Baker. Maybe you must hunt this vision, to *become it is finished*."

"That's so beautiful, so moving. Yes, to become *it is finished* without being finished, without completion. To hunt that fact every day means to remind myself every moment that it has been accomplished, *it is finished*. It's here. Now what?"

"Yes, now what? Do you have an answer to that question?"

After a pause, he says, "Ben, I'm telling you, all that is left are love songs to God. With all the world's conflict, motion, and noise, none of these things are as important as love for the one who accomplished everything. I'm going to write love song after love song to God."

"You're in your sixties, you have accomplished a great deal, and yet you're still willing to start over. Doesn't that feel daunting? Maybe even overwhelming?"

"I don't feel like I have a choice. I'm compelled."

"The world is full of artists who have tasted success and don't stay hungry."

"What do you mean by that word hungry?" he asks.

"I mean that they feel like they've arrived. For whatever reason, they've lost the drive to improve. The craft, the self-critique, the rigor—it all takes a backseat to their ego. Their work becomes derivative. They start listening to their own press."

"Yes, it's true. I fear that," he says.

"Alfred, Lord Tennyson's Ulysses says, 'I am become a name.' How awful to become a name, to become nothing more than your public persona. Fame is an oppressive thing."

He nods and says, "What did Rainer Maria Rilke say about that? Something like, 'Fame is but the sum of all the misunderstandings which gather about a name."

"How do you keep from letting those misunderstandings gather around your name?" I ask. "How do you keep fame from infecting your work?"

"Oh Ben, it terrifies me." He lifts his hands to shield himself and closes his eyes. "Keep it away from me. I don't want to hear it. Don't tell me that stuff. Don't do it." After a moment's reflection, he adds, "At the same time, I don't want to sound ungrateful. I'm very fortunate. Poetic fame, I mean, it's not much, but I feel lucky. What matters is the work."

"People imagine that a published poet is surrounded

by friends and a thousand demands. Is that true?"

"Actually, it's really scary and lonely out here. It's terrifying. And it's year after year of that kind of work."

"What do you mean by 'out here'?"

"I mean that place where the work can get done, that place inside me where I enter the pregnant darkness. Maybe I just don't like large groups of people. I don't know what I'm saying." He pauses again. "I just keep coming back to those three words—*it is finished*. If it's true that it is finished, then I'm free to live in those three words. The prayer of my life and my work has that much more meaning: *It is finished* makes me cry, *O my God. O my love. Holy, holy, holy*. Those are the attitudes of all great lyric poetry. All great poetry is some variation on those three themes. There are so many ways, so many inflections you can use to praise."

"Your prayer is interesting because many people fixate on one of those three. Some people are in awe of God, but they never come to love him. Some people love him but miss his holiness. Your prayer begins in awe and comes full circle. It forces me to pass from awe, to love, to reverence, and back to awe in a never-ending cycle."

"That's right. I want to hold onto this state of mind now that *it is finished*. It's the only thing that matters now."

"This revelation changes everything for you," I say. "Everything."

"Even how you see your father? You've written extensively about your conflicted relationship with him."

He gazes out over the park. Then he says, "My father was a big personality."

"He became a minister when your family came to the United States."

"Yes, a Presbyterian minister. People flocked to hear him. He used to fill the sanctuary like Billy Graham."

"He cast quite a shadow," I say. "Metaphorically speaking."

"I loved him. I remember he wanted me to learn to sing the song, 'God Bless The Child.' The Blood, Sweat and Tears version. He played the organ. I would sit there next to him and tell him it was hard, and he would say, 'You'll get it.' Do you know that song, Ben? It's a hard song to sing. He would get so mad sometimes when I didn't sing it right. Every Friday night, my brothers would rush out the door to play, and he would call me to practice with him. I didn't want to practice! Are you kidding me? But I would practice. And then it dawned on me that if I got too good at singing this song, he would take it on the road. No way was I going to do that. I remember telling my brothers that they were abandoning me. I was really mad. But they would say, 'Hey man, we love you for taking it! Thank you! He loves you best.' And they were right. I knew it, but man, it was hard."

"If he was Jacob, you were his Joseph. That song was his coat of many colors."

"Oh Ben, what a picture. It brings tears to my eyes. I think back, and I know that he loved me. Sometimes, when we got it right, when I was seated on the bench next to him and we were in rhythm, he would lean on me ever so gently."

"He could be quite tender at times."

"Tender, but volatile. It was hard to be his son. Certain afternoons, he would say, 'Get your notebook.' We would go on long drives, and he would dictate his sermon to me. But if I didn't have that notebook open and ready before he started talking, or if he saw me open that notebook after he had started talking, I was in trouble. He would get so mad. But if I did it right, he would talk, and I would copy it down. When he was onto something, he knew it and I knew it. Something beautiful happened. I didn't know you could read or encounter God at that level. When he was on like that, the whole world opened. When he was on, he would look at me and smile as if to say, 'You see it, right?

You see what's happening, right?' After those times, he would be good for days. He was so happy. But there were other days, man, when the revelation didn't come, and he couldn't find his way. He would stalk the vision like a hunting cat on those days, and nobody talked to him. He was scary, really scary. If you got in his way, watch out." Li-Young pauses, lost in thought. Then he says, "Poor man, poor man. He suffered."

"But you longed for his blessing. You hungered for it deeply."

"Yes, I really did."

"It's almost as if God has wired us with a longing to hear our fathers bless us. When we don't receive that blessing, there's a great heartache. When we do hear it, we feel at peace."

"I think that's right," he says.

"Your father hungered for revelation much like his son. In some respects, he has passed that longing down to you and now you get to live it out."

"That's true. He gave me a great gift. This is the revelation: *it is finished*. God is present. The Christic is all that matters. There's a sense of relief, but it doesn't eliminate the terror. The darkness is still dark, but it's infused with meaning now. It will be okay as long as God is at the center, but it's still a fearful thing."

"Like the disciples," I suggest, "when the sea was in turmoil and Jesus was sleeping in the boat's hull. They were afraid for their lives, so they woke Jesus so he would do something about it. When he told the sea to quiet down and the water immediately calmed, the disciples were terrified. They were afraid before, but now they were terrified because God was in the boat with them."

"So true. It's a terrible awe that's full of hope."

"Can we revisit something you said earlier? You said that once we realize *it is finished*, all that's left are love songs to God. What about poems that comment on issues in the world? Political poems? What about poems that rage against the way things are, or at least try to resolve those issues? Hasn't that been an important task for poets over the centuries?"

"Those poems are just litigations against the world," he says. "I love that stuff sometimes, but I also think there's another mode. All of that comes from a pre-*it is finished* mentality. Post-*it is finished*, none of those arguments with the world, arguments with community, arguments with God, matter."

"A few years ago, you said that many American poets come at their work with complaint, not praise, and so their poetry lacks richness and depth. You said, 'We should write out of grief, but not grievance. Grief is rich, ecstatic. But grievance is not—it's a complaint, it's whining.'That problem has only worsened over the last few years. At least, it seems so to me. Now we are catechizing our children in the doctrines of complaint. We're in a vicious cycle of complaint, rage, and self-destruction. It's the air we're breathing, so it's easy to start doing it, too. I wonder if you see any solution. Is there still hope for us?"

"We have forgotten how to praise anything but ourselves or our agendas," he says. "No wonder there are so many problems in the world. Forget yourself. Stop looking at yourself. Forget all of the grievance. The only thing left is love-talk to God."

"This is what Mary Magdalene understood when she broke the jar of expensive nard and anointed Christ's feet with it. While everyone else was talking politics, she gave herself to the moment. Gratitude spilled out of her. Is this what you mean?"

"Yes. That's it! My father preached a sermon on that story. She washes Christ's feet with her hair, right? The image itself is so powerful. The stillness embodied there. Christ is there, yes, but the entire scene is Christic. I suppose that every picture Christ enters becomes Christic. It becomes organized around the most spectacular, the greatest Good. That's what matters now. That's the only thing that matters, Ben. All that's left for me is to break the oil over his feet. All that's left are love songs to God."

From Blossoms
by Li-Young Lee

From blossoms comes
this brown paper bag of peaches
we bought from the boy
at the bend in the road where we turned toward
signs painted *Peaches*.

From laden boughs, from hands,
from sweet fellowship in the bins,
comes nectar at the roadside, succulent
peaches we devour, dusty skin and all,
comes the familiar dust of summer, dust we eat.

O, to take what we love inside,
to carry within us an orchard, to eat
not only the skin, but the shade,
not only the sugar, but the days, to hold
the fruit in our hands, adore it, then bite into
the round jubilance of peach.

There are days we live
as if death were nowhere
in the background; from joy
to joy to joy, from wing to wing,
from blossom to blossom to
impossible blossom, to sweet impossible blossom.

MAURICE MANNING

"Most people have the opportunity, at least at some point in their lives, to learn that living with frenzy is not something we have to do," he says. "There are plenty of experiences in our world that are the antidote to that. We can actually develop practices that strengthen those antidotes."

—*Maurice Manning*

I sat in on Maurice Manning's poetry workshop before our interview. It didn't take long to notice that he is one of those teachers who keeps trying to rope his students back from distraction, from their phones and laptops, with no guarantee of their attention. He did so repeatedly, kindly, often humorously, walking around to peer over their shoulder while they read their work or simply inviting them by name to offer something to the conversation. It struck me, while I was sitting there, that this is what Maurice (pronounced "Morris") Manning does in his poetry, too. He kindly, often humorously, ropes his readers back from life's distractions, whatever they might be.

Before we begin the interview, he gifts me with a recent publication of his poetry by Larkspur Press. I thank him and note the small volume's loveliness—its paper, binding, and print quality.

He says, "The man who runs Larkspur Press is named Gray Zeitz. When he was a young man, this is what he wanted to do, and he's been doing it for about fifty years. He operates a letterpress where all the letters are set by hand. He's got a big ol' machine that weighs a ton. He's so highly regarded that there are book collectors who will buy a copy of every book that he makes."

"I can see why," I say. Then, turning it over in my hands, I read his Author's Note aloud: "I began writing this during Lent of 2015 and during that season I determined that I no longer wish to think of any human being as my enemy." I look at him. He smiles.

"Your resolve must have been tested awful fierce during the last few years of societal and political upheaval," I say.

"Well, I'll tell you, we live near the site of the largest Civil War battle in Kentucky, the Battle of Perryville. A friend of mine told me a gory tale of when he was a boy in the early 1950s, while his parents were renovating a really old house. An old man came by and said he lived in that house during the Battle of Perryville and one day some soldiers came by with a wounded man on their horse. The soldiers asked if they could leave him with the family and his family obliged. The man had lost an arm and leg in the battle. They put the soldier up in the loft where he bled to death. That was the state of things. Nothing to do for the wounded but drop them hither and yon while you're running for your life. In the summer of 2015, I found part of a cannonball in my backyard. Finding the cannonball confirmed those local stories. So, you know, I started thinking about that. Of course, at that point in our country's history, we were marching toward twenty-first-century division. I had a realization. I wouldn't call it an epiphany; I would just call it a moment of clarity. I thought, why do we do this? Why do we divide ourselves? Does any good come of it? And I couldn't think of anything."

"A bit like the old-time family feuds that you write about, but on a larger scale," I say.

"Yes," he replies. "Much larger, and much more is at stake. I think when we war among ourselves, when we divide ourselves, everyone loses eventually. There might be a victor and a loser for a while, but we can't stay in that state. I find that very compelling."

"Maybe you could unpack that a little more," I say. "I'm thinking of your farm, for example, a place you love and want to tend well. You are encroached upon by wild animals or invasive species of plants. You want to create a space that is healthy and protected. How do you see that as different from unhealthy division?"

"Difference does not have to mean division, you know. In our woods, we have an American hornbeam tree growing next to a sugar maple. They're different, but they're growing out of the same soil. On the other hand, I didn't fence off my garden last year. As a consequence, the deer ate it all. This year, I'm going to put up a fence."

"I'm sure you will," I say.

"The deer will have plenty of other things to eat." He pauses. "I'm not trying to evade the question, but I think we impose artificial divisions. I don't know if those divisions actually, legitimately elevate one characteristic, one difference, over another."

"You're recognizing differences, but you're pulling back from a need for a hostile response to those differences. Is that it?"

"Yes, exactly. If division is based on hostility, then it doesn't serve anyone."

"There are differences between you and your students. You strike me as a teacher who walks alongside his students, tries to fight for them, and wards off the assault of their distractions. Do you see yourself in that position?"

"I would say that it's something I have had to adapt to. I've been teaching for twenty-four years. When I first started teaching, I thought the content was inherently valuable and I wouldn't have to prove its value to anyone. In more recent years, however, I've realized that what I must do is much bigger. In some ways, I'm in a position to help my students make connections and feel connected, to help them feel rooted in a society that is rootless. I can't fault them for their rootlessness, but I can pass along the value of connection and of accepting differences without flying off the handle."

"Actually," I add, "being able to talk about those differences in a healthy discourse is becoming a rare thing these days."

"Indeed."

"Speaking of being rooted, your poetry is very rooted in Kentucky. Is that a conscious choice? Or is it the consequence of being generationally rooted in Kentucky?"

"I just don't think I could do it any other way. I mean, I won't write about riding a subway because I don't ride on a subway. It's not part of my daily experience. One of the things that I have felt very lucky about is that for me, Kentucky is multiple things at once. By using Kentucky as a lens, I can look at aspects of human experience that go far beyond these geographical borders."

"Basically, you're telling me that I'm asking an apple tree why it chose to bear apples rather than pears."

"That's well put," he says, laughing. "It's still a useful question. I mean, someone was asked once whether he was a regional writer and he said, 'Well, isn't everyone?'

I mean, this is what you've got. This is what you've been given to write about."

"William Faulkner once said, 'I discovered that my own little postage stamp of native soil was worth writing about and that I would never live long enough to exhaust it, and that by sublimating the actual into the apocryphal I would have complete liberty to use whatever talent I might have to its absolute top.' He seems to share your leanings. Do you feel similarly?"

"I do indeed. I'm reading Faulkner right now. You know, I would never compare myself to Faulkner, but he's certainly someone I've learned from. Some of my books are full of personal experience in the here-and-now reality, but I've always been very interested in going beyond the material elements and moving toward a kind of mythology. Often, my poems have one foot in reality and one foot in the beyond. Part literal and part metaphorical."

"Let's talk about the mythology, the apocryphal nature of your poetry. One of my favorite attributes of your work is a kind of old-time, Daniel Boone, Paul Bunyan mythologizing of people who are really quite ordinary. Are those poems your attempt to honor some transcendent essence that goes unnoticed, something like what Gerard Manley Hopkins called an object's inscape?"

"I think I'm interested in the potential value of revisiting an experience that we thought about in one way and then, later, with the passage of time, we thought about it with greater significance. With the passage of time comes a dawning of a moment's significance."

"Is it fair to say that you're a gardener of memory, that you love to tend memory and see what blooms out of that soil?"

"Yes, that's a wonderful way of looking at it."

"You've shared that poetry wasn't part of your childhood. When did poetry woo you? I mean, if someone from the future had visited ten-year-old Maurice Manning and told him that he would one day be Writer in Residence at Transylvania University, the kid would have probably scoffed."

We laugh together and Manning says, "Well, listen now, you are correct, but let me tell you about this ink pen that I use." He removes the pen from his shirt pocket. "This belonged to my great-grandmother, who was the only person in any part of the family who read books. She wrote letters and postcards very dutifully. I often stayed with her. I remember she had this junk drawer and a pen in that junk drawer with no ink, but I would take that pen and I would take paper and make the action of writing even without ink because I associated writing with being serious and kind—because it was connected to my great-grandmother, who was serious and kind. Many years later, I was at a writing event. I was taking notes with a drugstore pen and a fellow author, Claudia Emerson, leaned over and she said, 'Don't you think you deserve to write with a more serious writing instrument?'"

We laugh.

"I thought to myself, okay, I'll have to take that under advisement. Her admonishments brought back the memory of this pen and I told her about my grandmother's pen. Well, a couple of weeks later, I received a package from Claudia and inside was a ballpoint version of this exact pen. She had no idea, of course. And so I called my mother to see if we had any of Great-Grandmother's things and, sure enough, among her belongings was this pen. So I bought some ink and filled it and I've been using it ever since."

"Has the pen, the fact that it belonged to your great-grandmother, changed your interaction with your poetry while you write?"

"Yes, it's made me value the privilege of writing much more."

"I have my great-grandfather's carpentry pencil," I say. "It's just a stub. It was a stub when it was given to me. But what a strange feeling to realize that I'm deeply honored to have this thing that isn't special, apart from the fact that it belonged to my great-grandfather. Maybe that's an appreciation gained with age."

Manning nods. "Think of all the work he did with that pencil," he says.

"And I think of his spirit that chose to pick up the pencil and use it to build something," I add. "It's not just about the pencil; it's about what that pencil represents. I want the same persistent spirit in my work."

"Indeed."

"You came to fatherhood late in life, which is its own joy and terror."

"Yes, yes it is." He laughs and looks out the window.

"How has that experience shaped you as a poet? What has that little lady done to you?"

"Lots. I feel time more acutely, you know. She'll be relatively young when I die. I won't be there to guide her or comfort her or be an actual companion to her. The books have the potential to be a companion to her, I suppose. It's very likely that my little girl will know me more through my writing than through actual interaction with me. That thought is almost too overwhelming to consider for very long. She's a gift."

"Does it add urgency to writing poetry?"

"No. I don't feel any rush. Probably the worst thing you can do as a poet is rush. It usually doesn't go well."

"Your little girl is going to grow up in a politically charged climate. How do you see poetry serving her and others who might feel awash in conflict, anxiety, the unknown?"

"Most people have the opportunity, at least at some point in their lives, to learn that living with frenzy is not something we have to do," he says. "There are plenty of experiences in our world that are the antidote to that. We can actually develop practices that strengthen those antidotes. I often suggest to students that they learn to identify twenty-five species of trees by their leaf, bark, and branch system. Then learn to do the same thing with songbirds and wildflowers. Learn their local names. I'm not suggesting that everyone become naturalists in a scientific way, in a bookish sense, but in a human way. I would like them to relate to the world around them relationally."

"When my wife and I bought a piece of land a few years ago, I found myself feeling a little bereft," I say. "I realized that I didn't know the plants or the flowers or the birds. I longed to have a name for these new companions. It's one thing to enjoy the quiet and being present in nature, but being able to name the plants and animals around me changes the relationship just as it does with people. I may notice that you are present with me in this room, but knowing your name changes our relationship. When you suggest learning the names of plants and animals, you're drawing our attention to another layer of relationship."

"Yes. You know, for too many people, nature is the backdrop for humanity. But we are integrated with it. We are totally dependent on nature, even if we don't think we are. You would think we would take better care of it. And, to go back to a previous point in this discussion, we are totally dependent upon each other as human beings. We are kidding ourselves if we think otherwise. We need each other, even if we don't like each other. There's no doubt about it."

"You grew up reading the Bible. How does your faith inform or interact with your poetry writing?"

"They definitely interact. I guess I'm hesitant to say, you know, that writing a poem is the same as praying. Writing a poem might be preliminary to praying. Passing through a poetic mood might be necessary for me to enter a time of prayer."

"Is that because the attention required to write a poem is required in prayer?"

"That's some of it," he replies. "You know, writing

a poem requires language, words. For me, prayer is an effort to go beyond words."

"Something like when Scripture says that the Holy Spirit hears our groaning, that the Holy Spirit translates our wordless ache?" I ask.

"Exactly. A poem is too anchored in human reality. The spiritual effort is to reach a spiritual reality that transcends the human and, in some ways, is inexplicable to the human mind."

"Would you say that the Christian faith of your youth runs parallel to your poetry? I'm not simply referring to Christian doctrine; it's more than that. What is their relationship?"

"Well, I was raised a Christian. I attend a Christian church. In my experience, my poetry and the Christian religion definitely run parallel. In poetry, though, I can ask questions about the religious. I can voice hesitation or skepticism. The poem can ask the question, but it can't provide the answer. Religion might be able to answer the question, but not always. You know, daily experience invites us to profound encounters that we may not actually understand. The poem can only point that out. It can't resolve anything. Poetry can highlight our dilemma, but it can't resolve what religion resolves."

"In your book of poems, *One Man's Dark*, you have these Job-like moments when you ask God really frank questions. These are honest interlocutions, but they don't resolve the ambiguity. It's hard to live in ambiguity, but poetry requires that a little bit."

"It does. You know, my students are pre-programmed to oppose ambiguity, but I tell them that very often the subjects of poetry and even of art are ambiguous. Maybe that's one reason why we need art. It helps us encounter ambiguity in terms that deepen us."

"Your poetry leans toward the quiet beauty of creation. Do you feel a need to point our eyes toward those things?"

"I've never wanted my poetry to preach," he says. "As far as my experience goes, the quiet beauty of a natural place is soothing, but not just that. It's way more than that. It is the surest way to understand that we belong to the natural order. When I walk in the woods, I stop thinking of myself. I don't worry about anything in my immediate circumstance. In some ways, my so-called self ceases to matter in any way at all because I am fully integrated in something bigger than myself. I'm as integrated as the moss on the tree or the wildflowers perking up in the leaf matter. I find it a great comfort to sense that I belong here just as the violet belongs here."

"Okay, we've been very serious, but we should talk about your podcast," I say. "How did that come into the world?"

"Ha, all right. Let's see," he replies, "it was during the pandemic in 2020, and I suddenly had more time on my hands. I was aware that many people, including some of my friends, needed some laughter, so I decided to write a bunch of goofy poems and share those poems with my friends who felt worried and threatened. In the Appalachian region there's a tradition of tall tales called Jack tales. The characters are larger than life and the events are completely outrageous, but they're presented as if they're totally normal. So I wrote a bunch of these Jack tales. I found out there was state arts council funding available and I applied for it. Though I had never heard a podcast before, I told them I was going to make a podcast. So my friend—a man who understands the technology involved—and I started *The Grinnin' Possum Podcast*. It's a bit of a local idiom. The possum is a trickster in Appalachian folklore. We did ten episodes, and eventually we started traveling the state to record episodes at interesting locations with live audiences. We recorded one of these episodes at an old church called the Old Mud Meeting House. It's a church built in the 1800s. The acoustics are the most interesting

I've ever heard. We added a fiddle player and a mandolin player. Each episode has a goofy poem or two, a couple of old-time songs, and a little bit of the local history. Honestly, it doesn't feel like we're performing. It feels like we're enjoying something together as a community."

"Humor pervades your work. It's often subtle in your poetry, but in this podcast, it's overt. Would you say that humorous poetry is a cathartic release for you? Or is it the little boy inside who keeps coming out?"

He laughs. "It's more the latter. I know that the present circumstances of the world are grim, but I can't help but find humor. I love to laugh. I love cutting up with other people. Sometimes it doesn't take other people; I'll just do it on my own." He laughs again.

"Okay, final question. How would you conclude the following: 'Dear Poet…' Your answer can be quite open. You could address dead poets, living poets, even poets not yet born."

"Alright, I guess I would say, 'Dear poet, I hope you recognize that what you do is a privilege, and I hope you enjoy it. Enjoy the work.'"

"Whether it gets published or not."

"Correct. Appreciate what you do for what it is."

Morning and Evening I Shall Drink the Dew
by Maurice Manning

It's not an effort but a fact
that time stops being time,
and there's nothing left to realize
because the mind at last belongs
to the landscape where it is,
like the root of an ironwood tree
plunging into the spongy ground
with moss and sorrel and nameless green
above, and warbling birdsong
singing before first light.
There's nothing for the mind to think,
nothing to do, and no awareness
to piddle with. Now that's one of
the biggest follies ever to stroll
in the shade of folly, to be aware
to the point of being too aware.
You have to forget yourself and belong
to a world you grasp imperfectly
and partly as a dream that's not
your dream at all. It's where the loved
ones all have gone—your father's horse,
the storytellers and those in the story,
the singing voice you've always heard,
the rivers, the woods, the green, the birds,
the beginning and end of you and time,
and then, and then, you make it rhyme.

PAUL
MARIANI

"The poet must enter the poem, must be somehow there in the poem, spending his or her blood as the words flow out and on. And this, my friend, cannot be faked. The perceptive reader will spot it and the interchange will end. Now, this is true of all real poetry. But the poet who seriously invokes the Scriptures has an added obligation to meet the words found there and create a music that will serve as a worthy diadem for that diamond. And that will come at a cost, a struggle."

—*Paul Mariani*

When I started interviewing poets of faith in January 2024, I asked a publisher for suggestions. He immediately mentioned Paul Mariani, calling him an "elder statesman of contemporary poetry that engages faith." That's not the kind of praise I hear very often, so it gave me pause. I had read Mariani before, but his significance had been unknown to me. I asked the publisher if he would elaborate.

This is what the publisher wrote: "Well, in the late 1980s Paul had already established himself as a leading poet and biographer of poets, but he took a risk by starting to write and publish poems that directly engaged with his Catholic faith. You have to understand that this was still in a time when the major gatekeepers of the culture were militantly anti-religious. He demonstrated that you could be a major literary figure in the midst of the mainstream public square and be a person of faith—at a time when many Christians preferred to huddle in a subculture."

This helped me realize that Paul Mariani has been doing the hard spadework necessary for cultural cultivation long before I started writing. Truth be told, I have been the beneficiary of his work for many years now.

Thinking through his life's work, it was difficult for me to choose whether to ask him about his own poetry or to discuss his formidable efforts at writing about other poets. I decided to split the difference.

"You seem to have twin engines that propel your work: a love for poetic expression and a love for poets," I say. "When were those seeds planted?"

"Well, when it comes to writing poetry," he replies, "I wrote my first poem in the spring of 1957. I was training to join the Marianist teaching order, living in community, sleeping in a large dorm each night along with about forty other novices, attending morning Mass (said in Latin back then), and being fed by a small group of German nuns who lived across the way. One day, another order of local nuns posted a poetry contest for a religious poem about Lent or Easter. I asked Brother Clyde if he could help me write a sonnet on the Passion of Christ. He couldn't, he said, but he directed me to a battered book of poems that contained definitions in the back about poetic forms. I sat down and studied the forms, figured out the intertwining of the rhymed lines and the nature of the five iambs. Over the next several days, I hammered out three quatrains and titled it "Forgive Me."

I help to beat and scourge Your back a crimson red
And place a crown of prickly thorns upon Your regal head.
Your sacred name and character I mock and ridicule.
O Lord each time I flee Your love I prove myself a fool.

I hurt and help to make You fall along the Dolor's way
And scorn Your mother and the others as they watch and pray.
I strip Your garment from Your limbs and from Your whip-lashed skin.
Yes, all of this I do to You when I commit a sin.

I help to drive the ugly nails into Your feet and wrists
And mock Your kingly deity with sland'rous waving fists.
Each time I sin against Thee, Lord, I help to break Your heart.
Lord, help me hate my sins and evermore from them depart!

"I'm glad you still have the poem," I say. "Did you win?"

"The good nuns awarded me with a ten-dollar first-place prize. I spent that money on a beautiful rosary for my mother."

"Tell me about your mother."

"Both my parents dropped out of high schools on the upper East Side when each turned sixteen, thanks to the Great Depression. My father delivered carloads of food by truck and horse-drawn wagon. My mother lost her father in France, where he was mustard gassed on the northern front when she was nine. My mother was a week shy of her seventeenth birthday when she had me."

"How many siblings did you have?"

"I am the oldest of seven siblings. I know my mother did the best she could, taking care of the seven of us while working nights at the publishing houses down in Garden City, and drinking to medicate herself against my father's outbursts of rage. Sad to say, but there it is. Once, he wanted to pull me out of school at sixteen to work full-time in his gas station, but my mother, who knew I had unusual learning skills, said that would only happen over her dead body. Thank God for mothers like that."

"Amen. You obviously never entered the priesthood."

"Pretty soon after I wrote that poem, I decided that I wanted to get married and have a family of my own.

At Manhattan College in the Bronx, I took as much religion, literature, philosophy, Latin, Greek, and history as I could. My father wanted me to pursue a 'respectable' course of study, like engineering or law, to make sure I made a decent living. But I kept returning to English, and decided at the last minute to major in that."

"So you discovered the poets at Manhattan?"

"It was only in my last semester at Manhattan, in the spring of '62, that I discovered my first great love: the Jesuit poet Gerard Manley Hopkins. Here was a Catholic poet who radically redirected poetry, and who had a profound impact on me and many other poets. I think I have always been influenced by the sacramental nature of beauty, and how it can manifest itself in the stress and music of language. While he published virtually nothing in his forty-four years of life, he kept writing. It took his close friend, Robert Bridges, thirty years after Hopkins's death to finally publish Hopkins's poems in a slim volume. There's so much to love and admire in Hopkins's work."

"You've written about Hopkins extensively."

"I've published two books on Hopkins, the first being my heavily-reworked dissertation under the guidance of the great Dante scholar and poet, Allen Mandelbaum, which Cornell University brought out in early 1970. And then, thirty-eight years later, in 2008, *Gerard Manley Hopkins: A Life*, published by Viking/Penguin.

"Do you have a favorite Hopkins poem?" I ask.

"Although I admire them all," he says, "my favorite is 'The Windhover,' the sonnet Hopkins wrote in late May of 1877 as he prepared for his ordination to the priesthood. He dedicated this Petrarchan sonnet to his hero, 'Christ our Lord.' You'll notice how the first eight lines all rhyme on the word 'king'—four with a strong stress (*king, wing, swing, thing*) and four with unaccented syllables (*riding, striding, gliding, hiding*). It sounds like the lift and fall of the windhover's wings as it flies into the winds off the hills of northern Wales.

I caught this morning morning's minion, king-
     dom of daylight's dauphin, dapple-dawn-drawn Falcon,
     in his riding
Of the rolling level underneath him steady air, and striding
High there, how he rung upon the rein of a wimpling wing
In his ecstasy! then off, off forth on swing,
     As a skate's heel sweeps smooth on a bow-bend: the hurl
     and gliding
     Rebuffed the big wind. My heart in hiding
Stirred for a bird, – the achieve of, the mastery of the thing!

Then, in the final six lines, we watch as the windhover buckles and drops to the ground. It is Christ in the Incarnation, Christ as he falls and sacrifices himself for us. It's a sacrifice far lovelier and more dangerous than anything before—the way a plough with sheer plod cuts through the dirt and turns up thousands of speckled quartz pieces, previously hidden, but now shining for us to see. Or the way those blue-bleak embers in the fire grate break through the iron grating and—as they fall—gall themselves (think of the vinegar gall pushed up to the crucified Christ's lips as he was dying) and gash gold-vermilion: his blood turned to the gold of our ransom.

Brute beauty and valour and act, oh, air, pride, plume, here
    Buckle! AND the fire that breaks from thee then, a billion
Times told lovelier, more dangerous, O my chevalier!

No wonder of it: shéer plód makes plough down sillion
Shine, and blue-bleak embers, ah my dear,
    Fall, gall themselves, and gash gold-vermilion.

"In *The Mystery of It All*, you wrote that Hopkins pleaded with God for the 'peace that came with writing not for himself…or *The New York Times*. …He hoped from now on to sweat out his writing at God's dictation.' Do you share that hope? How do we prevent the allure to write for something other than merely the humble dictation of the Spirit's work in us?"

"I do share that hope. Since I believe that the gift of writing poetry has been a blessing from God, it is that grace to which I return whenever I undertake to write a poem: the Holy Spirit as Muse. What did Hopkins say? 'Jesus Christ is the only true literary critic.' I'm grateful for all the rest, but that focus remains the true north."

"What is the hardest hurdle you've had to overcome as a writer?"

"Here was the issue for me: not just to write, but to write what I wanted to write about. As a college professor, I soon learned to take the axiom 'publish or perish' seriously. But I also felt a responsibility and a deep drawing to write about the underlying sacramental tensions in the daily mysteries we encounter. Hopkins understood this, Flannery O'Connor understood it. So did Denise Levertov, Robert Lowell, John Berryman, Hart Crane, and Wallace Stevens."

"Hopkins struggled mightily with insecurities about his poetic work," I say. "It seems to me that those feelings are common among poets. Have you felt that inadequacy too, especially given the weightiness of a sacramental vision?"

"Yes," he replies. "Lynda Kong recently wrote in *Mockingbird* magazine, 'I didn't know how to pay tribute to such a great God, or to register the complicated and contradictory experiences of being a Christian with my measly words, my dull words. …I didn't know how to offer a new voice, in a new century. I was intimidated.' I understand her sense of trying to sing in the shadow of one's predecessors. But you must venture out and try to write what you believe you were meant to write. And you look for those poets who seem to speak to you directly and learn what each of those poets can teach you—inscape, beauty, daring, the American idiom. You get knocked down—the dark angel somewhere in the rafters laughing at you——then you get up, and you go forward again. And you do what you can. And somehow the light breaks through again, thank God."

"It seems to me that your later poetry is addressed more and more to friends—those still living and those who live in your memory. Is poetry a way for you to hold onto memories as you age, to keep those you love alive in your heart?"

"That's beautifully phrased. Yes, more and more of my later poems are addressed to friends and family—the polestars of my life—to thank them. And, of course, there's my immediate family: my dear wife Eileen, a game changer ever since that evening I met her at a college gathering (me from Manhattan College, she from St. John's University) in a bar in Mineola, New York back in December 1959. And then my three sons, and our grandkids and their jokes at their grandfather's expense. I can't think of any greater blessing than breaking bread with them at family gatherings. Truly, they have made all the difference to my life. There are also poems for my mother and father, poems both sad and happy. And of course, my six younger siblings."

"You refer to your time as poetry editor at *America* magazine as a time when you saw a great deal of poetry that lacked spiritual dimension. You saw poems that were strong on religious sensibility and the verse forms were strong, but the poetry was lacking. Can you elaborate on what you mean? Is the problem a shallow spiritual life culture-wide? Is it because we have become unmoored from the Scriptures? How do we write poems that are more than simply religious, poems that lift us into another spiritual dimension?"

"Good question, Ben. And a difficult one as well. Many religious poets seem to think that if they just fill the lines with quotations or hints of quotations from the Bible, then that will suffice. It will not. Nor will the poem that uses poetic formulae—a sonnet, a cinquain, a triolet, a sestina, heroic couplets, the ballad form, and so on—result in a satisfactory poem touching on the spiritual dimension. Certainly not a Catholic poem. As Emily Dickinson said, it's only when the hair on your head seems to respond that you are in the presence of the real poem. Personally, I read poetry every day, but only rarely do I feel I am in the presence of a poem that truly matters."

"So much depends upon the caliber of the person writing the poem, doesn't it?"

"Here's one thing for sure: the poet herself or himself must enter the poem, must be somehow there in the poem, spending his or her blood as the words flow out and on. And this, my friend, cannot be faked. The perceptive reader will spot it and the interchange will end. Now, this is true of all real poetry. But the poet who seriously invokes the Scriptures has an added obligation to meet the words found there and create a music that will serve as a worthy diadem for that diamond. And that will come at a cost, a struggle."

"In *The Mystery of It All*, you describe Scott Cairns as one of those poets who offers 'grasshopper transcendency, the momentary lift or epiphany, in which the spiritual dimension is, for a moment, glimpsed before it disappears.' What is that evasive thing you are talking about?"

"William Carlos Williams wrote a magnificent epic American poem, 'Paterson.' There's a passage where the poet walks across the park on Garret Mountain and notices the grasshoppers leaping into the air, their wings catching the sunlight for a moment so that they seem transformed, and then quickly settling back into the high grass. I have taken that to mean that momentary lift, that epiphany, in which something is for a moment glimpsed before it disappears. It can be the shimmering silence—that radiant white space, a momentary lifting of the spirit, something akin to the silences between and among and in and through those sounds transformed into musical cadences. The thing that returns us again and again to the mystery of the well-wrought poem."

"Your comments remind me of Paul's words in his first letter to the Corinthians, when he writes, 'For now we see in a mirror dimly, but then face to face. Now I know in part; then I shall know fully, even as I have been fully known.'"

"Yes, that's exactly it," he replies. "The best poems give us a peek into something most of us—if we are attentive enough, the way the poet must be—grasp now only momentarily. It's a blessing, a gift, a grace the poet offers, something the poet catches in the shadow of the sun—a gift from the good Lord for which the only real response would be a profound thank you."

"You're talking about a glimpse of light, or hope, or redemption."

"Yes. I'm not speaking here of the poets of darkness, of whom there are plenty, thank you. I've been there, taught them, tried to understand them, in a sense, to even out the field. But they are little help to me, especially as I grow older. My journey here is coming to a close, whether I like it or not, so what can I do but acknowledge the darkness and search, search for the light? My Catholic faith is essential in this search. It helps me to accept grace and give that grace back to others in whatever ways I can. It helps me listen to others, acknowledging their pain, rejoicing in their joy, accepting love and giving that love back in the written word."

"You've been doing that for a long time," I say.

"It's been seventy years since my first poem—followed by biographies, memoirs, critical essays, reflections, and more poems. But each time I write, I must face the blank page. And then I begin with a line, and then another, and, perhaps the next day, another and another, in the end surprising myself, if not my Creator."

"That's a wonderful answer, Paul. I think it has become a full-time job to hang on to hope, especially as we age. I'm thankful for your example in that regard. When it's all said and done, what do you hope you have accomplished in your life? What are several things you believe your life has testified to?"

"When I look back on my youth growing up on New York's East 51st Street back in the 1940s," he says, "I find myself lucky first of all to be alive. Those were tough years. I nearly lost my feet when I was three and tried to take a bath in the kitchen sink early one morning just after my father had left for work, and the hot water scalded both my feet badly. If it hadn't been for a new wonder drug called penicillin, the only option would have been to amputate both my feet at the ankles. And then there was the time when I was six, returning alone in the late December dark after going by myself to see Walt Disney's *Song of the South*. A teenager named Harry and his gang cornered me and poured kerosene around my feet—they'd been burning Christmas trees tossed out onto the streets—and then lit matches and taunted me. I cried and shouted, but no one would help me, not even a gentleman slouching around the gang and minding his own business. My mother came running up the street shouting, my little brother in tow and my sister in the baby carriage. My father took care of that the next morning when he confronted Harry's family, knocked Harry's older brother just home from jail across the room, and told Harry's father, sitting there silently, to make sure Harry stayed away from me."

"You have survived a great deal."

"I suppose that's true. But I'm not alone," he replies. "Like most people, I'm a survivor. I have no hearing in my right ear—a condition I was born with—and so I've had to work hard to make sure I hear what someone says to me, and teaching classes and seminars for over half a century has often been a challenge. But you go into the class, welcome all of your students, joke if you can, and listen carefully to what they say. The benefit of that is that I'm a good listener, and I listen attentively to what someone says. I'm also a Catholic Christian, so there was always this sense of hope that the good Lord would be there for me, and I would try to bear witness to that. Which is why I chose the name Christopher—Christ Bearer—for my confirmation name.

Years later, in 1975, I served as rector at a retreat and was in the makeshift room where we kept the tabernacle with the Eucharist. I could hear Christ prompting me,

'Go ahead, Paul, ask for what's in your heart now.' I answered that I was fully satisfied with the work my team had done in witnessing and that was sufficient. But again, the prompting: 'Go ahead, ask.' And I said, 'Well, Lord, if it is your will, help me to be a poet, dedicated to you, lifting you up in ten thousand ways we find in what we call the ordinary.' And within a year, I had somehow managed to complete an entire book of poems, my first, called *Timing Devices*—poems that would leave an impact. If you look at the list of books I've published over the past half century—spiritual memoirs, essays, critical texts, those six biographies, and a thousand pages of my own poetry, it does amount to a bounty, thanks to the good Lord and the patience and support of my dear wife of sixty years, Eileen—truly a blessing for me.

"You described Eileen as a game changer. Tell me more about her."

"When I look across the table at her, I realize that none of what I've done would have been possible without her. I don't know, but it seems we men often take for granted what our women do to keep the home together and functioning—the daily chores of shopping and preparing meals, raising a family, and then being there for the next generation as well. Truly, as I meditate on this, I see in those meals—in that breaking of the bread—an incredible abundance of love and grace. Of course, she's been there in all the good times and the bad times, even, to tell the truth, when I wasn't there for her. For many years she typed out all my writings, my dissertation, drafts of essays and poems. And she has read everything I've written over a lifetime. She has always made astute insights into what I've written."

"She's a wonderful poem herself. Okay, final question. How would you finish the following: 'Dear Poet...'"

"Well, I would probably speak to all the poets with whom I've journeyed over the past sixty years. There's Father Hopkins, of course. And there's my beloved Dante. And Bill Williams with his search for the American idiom. And the brilliance of Stevens and Crane. And those early years especially Lowell, as he knitted the warp and woof of Hopkins and John Milton into his 'Quaker Graveyard in Nantucket' and then later the brutal honesty of 'Skunk Hour' as his majestic vision collapsed, only to have to be rebuilt as he could, in spite of his mental travails. Then add my dear Miss Dickinson and Elizabeth Bishop, Mary Oliver, Marie Howe, Gwendolyn Brooks, Langston Hughes, Claude McKay, Robert Hayden, and Wilfred Owen.

And William Butler Yeats and Seamus Heaney, both of whom I taught in seminars."

"That's amazing," I reply.

"Well, there's a long list of poets for whom I'm grateful," he says. "Bob Pack, Phil Levine, Eddie Hirsch, Garrett Hongo, Scott Cairns, and my dear friend Martín Espada. I shouldn't forget to mention the greats: Geoffrey Chaucer, Shakespeare, Virgil, Homer, Sappho. You can see where this is going. Well, I say, thank you. Thank you all for a rich and bountiful life filled with poetry."

Elegy for Emely
by Paul Mariani

Once more the leaves are falling. Summer's
gone like some evicted tenant, and the light
we loved keeps fading with each day. The sun
clicks left a little more each evening, and the bright

notes of jays and finches that flocked last week
about our feeders have left for warmer climes.
And so it goes, as it has forever. And as the light
grows shorter, those crickets that kept time

with the katydids have packed up their strings
and violas and departed. And now my dear
sister lies sleeping in her bed three thousand
miles away, the morphine flowing through her

as her family and the nurse attend her needs
while the hours and weeks drone on and on.
Our lone warrior has grown silent now, tucked tight
in her cocoon. And still, come dawn, her big brown

baby eyes seem fixed on me again, her oldest brother,
as I keep peering through the crib bars there
in our dingy fifth-floor walkup on East Fifty-first,
the clop of horses and the El melding into prayer.

The war's finally over now, and Daddy's home again,
and peace, the papers say, is flowing everywhere.
But your wide eyes keep staring into mine,
as if to ask, "Brother, can you tell me why we're here?"

Questions I couldn't answer then, and, dear sister,
cannot answer now. But here we are, for the time
we've been allotted. And questions too which ask
what might have been, if . . . If only what? I climb

back now sixty years and more, and once again
catch you staring into a void I cannot see
that winter night I staggered back into the kitchen,
having begged our mother to shut off the engine, weak

as she was, and come inside, in silence and defeat,
our father for once speechless, and you there
in the doorway, your eyes announcing it was
over now, that one day you'd move away from here,

which in time was what you did. And now, after
all these years, as you lie sleeping in your bed,
you're moving on to another place only you can know,
the cancer having won, which took Mom and Dad,

and if that wasn't quite enough, our youngest sister too.
Each day now, sweet Emely, I pray you find the light
and peace you longed for, your feathers unfolding now,
our eyes fixed fast on you, as you begin your final flight.

MARILYN
NELSON

"There are miracles happening all the time. If you're not noticing them or grateful for them when they're small, how will you notice them when they're immense? Gratitude is part of the price you pay for existence. It's not hard, but it's terribly important."

—*Marilyn Nelson*

Marilyn Nelson wrote that when she discovered poetry as a child, "it was like soul-kissing, the way the words filled my mouth." In the years since, she has not lost that intimacy with words, with life itself. It has been my impression that she holds life in her mouth so she can taste its many flavors. Even in my initial greeting, she expressed that wonderful eagerness.

"I'm so grateful for the chance to meet you, Marilyn," I say. "Thank you for being willing to spend some time with me."

She laughs and says, "Well, thank you, but sometimes you don't know where conversations will go. Who knows what surprises or ideas a conversation will bring? I have this little notebook, just in case."

"I can't wait to be surprised together," I say. "Let's start with your faith journey. You were born in 1946.

Your father was a Tuskegee Airman and served in the United States Air Force. Your mother was a teacher and pianist. Was church a part of your growing up?"

"Military life means you move around a lot, so we didn't have a home church," she says. "I grew up attending the Protestant chapel on base. I remember having a pre-teen crush on one of my Sunday school teachers. He was a lieutenant from Montana or Wyoming. In fact, I recently searched the internet for him and found that he is known for his Christian service and commitment. I was glad to hear that. When I was in high school, my mother joined a Lutheran church in California. It was a little church that decided to integrate when the neighborhood became racially diverse, which, as you know, was uncommon for a church to do in those days. So I became a Lutheran. Over the years, I became known by those in leadership as a smart African American who was interested in poetry, so they invited me to work on a Lutheran hymnal. My Lutheranism is deep and long-lasting."

"So your faith has traveled with you through life."

"Well, mostly, I suppose. I don't think one's faith journey is a straight line. It's a meandering, confusing maze. I've been thinking lately about the phrase 'accepting the nos.' You beg God for something and he says no. It's hard to accept the nos. It leaves you with many questions."

"Indeed, and some are harder to accept than others."

"Yes, exactly. Some of them change the entire direction of your life or your sense of who you are."

"You've had many life-changing experiences. What were some of those when you were younger?"

"I spent the summer of 1967 in Chicago," she says. "Dr. Martin Luther King, Jr. moved the Civil Rights Movement north that year. I supported myself by working with a little community organization on the west side of Chicago and spent whatever time I could get free marching. It was a summer of marching. It was also a summer of revelation for me. One of those revelations was the unmasking of the human heart. We would march by a little church on a Sunday morning. I remember the doors opening and people filing out. Little old ladies with gray hair walking out to the sidewalk where we were mostly praying, you know? And they would spit at us and yell sexual profanities. I was shocked. I didn't even know what these things meant. And I remember Dr. King standing at the front of the line, reminding us that ours was the power of love and that we needed to find that power."

"You don't soon forget experiences like that."

"No, you don't. They still come to mind quite often."

"You would have been around twenty or twenty-one years old, right? That's a formative time of life."

"Yes, indeed."

"Over the years, I've wondered if people kept God's law as He intended—if we treated each other the way God told us to treat each other—would racism go away?"

"Maybe," she says. "All I know is that this hostility we see around the world today has been with us from the very beginning, brother against brother—from Cain and Abel all the way to the crucifixion. That's what the Bible shows us. I grew up with probably ninety percent white kids because we were a military family. What I learned from my time in Chicago is that those kids had to make conscious decisions to be my friend. One of my best friends from middle school was a wonderful white girl named Kim. I used to sleep over at her house, eat dinner with her family. I remember camping out on their driveway." She laughs. "Kim told me years later that she had to fight with her parents to be my friend. I never dreamed of that possibility. She covered it up, but so did they. Eating dinner with them at least once a week, I never saw a hint of it. I'm not sure what to make of all of that, but it was a revelation to me."

"Was she fighting her parents because she knew it was right? Or was it because of something less complex?"

"I think she wasn't doing anything more than just being a friend to her friend. To make it larger than that is to assume that a young child can generalize. I don't think that's what it was about. You know, in friendship, you give your affection away and it becomes a commitment. How can you turn your back on that commitment? In the long run, it's these little decisions of love that matter most."

"In an interview once, you said that every day is a portal to the rest of your life. Could you explain?"

"I'm afraid I have no memory of the context in which I said that."

I laugh. "You don't have all of your interviews memorized?"

"I'm afraid not, but it certainly sounds good. I suppose every moment is a portal into the future. There's no way of knowing what that future holds, but I feel that probably the best thing to do is find reasons for gratitude in every moment. There are miracles happening all the time. If you're not noticing them or grateful for them when they're small, how will you notice them when they're immense? Gratitude is part of the price you pay for existence. It's not hard, but it's terribly important."

"These little miracles are not hard to see," I say, "we're just not practiced at noticing."

"A few years ago, I read a prayer called, I think, 'The Prayer of the Loving Gaze.' That's all it is, putting your love into your eyes as you look around at the world, at people, at everything. To see with a loving gaze. Gratitude is an entry, a portal into a rewarding life. That's why people who have nothing can be as filled with gratitude as those who have abundant stuff. The gratitude comes from you, not from your circumstances."

"You're touching on a topic that has come up quite often in my conversations with poets. When I started this journey, I didn't have an agenda. I just wanted to meet these poets. I suspected, however, that they might help me grow in gratitude. My favorite poets have gratitude in their eyes. They have love for the details of life. I wonder if that's particularly common with poets."

"That's an interesting question," she says. "If you're any kind of an artist, you know what it's like to have something not only come *to* you, but *through* you. When you have experienced that kind of an epiphany, when you write something that taught you something in the process, then you can only be humble and grateful to have received such a gift."

"To be effective, you have to remain surprised and amazed by what comes through your pen."

"I once heard an interview with a great classical composer. He said that he only writes the music that he hears." She laughs. "But how can you hear something that didn't exist until you wrote it down? It's a marvel."

"Says Marilyn Nelson, who writes moving poems that come to her, but she can't explain where they came from. You only write the music that you hear, too."

"Well, right now, Marilyn Nelson hopes to hear the music again someday. Poems seem to have gone on strike for now."

"I'm sorry to hear that. Have you had many seasons in your life when the poems dried up?"

"I have, but this feels different. I think this is connected to age more than anything. When I was younger and those dry spells came, I would accept it and give it an end date. I would say, 'I'm not going to write for three months,' or something. It became a kind of Lenten fast. I've even taken vows of silence sometimes for that reason. But usually by the time the specified limits have been reached, I've got it again, but not this time."

"To take a farming metaphor, you were letting the soil rest."

"Yes, exactly."

"Do you feel vulnerable and a little anxious by this part of the aging process?"

"Well, yes. In my family, if you reach the age of sixty-five, then you're on your last mental legs. I'm seventy-eight, so every time I don't remember a word—everyone says it's normal, I know—I feel anxious."

"My grandmother was fond of saying that aging is not for the faint of heart."

"Right, it's entirely not," she replies.

"Some writers feel more poetic when things are going poorly than when things are going well. Is joy less inspirational?"

"I don't know how to answer that question. My writing tends to be based on research. It tends to be about lives that are not my own life, so I can fall in love with the subject matter. I can write through the experience as an imaginative act. I'm thinking of my work on George Washington Carver and other historical characters."

"Yusef Komunyakaa says you are the kind of writer who is rooted in the basic soil of redemptive imagination. I think he means that, like with gratitude, you are angling for redemption in your work. Even if you're writing about difficult things, you're not just leaving us in that awful moment."

"I suppose that's what I'm trying to do when I write. I have been lucky in having been given subject matter that is redemptive. Some people have other subject matters to write about. My own life has been a good life. I think about what so many people have to deal with, so much suffering in the world. How can I, sitting here with my three cats and listening to a bird chirp in a tree, complain about anything? I have been so blessed."

An airplane flies low overhead so we have to stop talking. When it passes, she laughs and says, "Except for when airplanes fly over the top of me while I'm talking to people."

"Ah yes, the joys of living near an airport."

"But even these airplanes remind me of my childhood living on the Air Force base. I used to love hearing those planes when I was a little girl because every plane in the sky could have been my father flying up there to protect us. You know, that was my world. Daddy was up there taking care of us. Goodness, I should write a poem about that."

"You had a wonderful relationship with your dad."

"Yes, I did."

"In a world devastated by father hunger, you seem to be one of the lucky few who had a good one."

"We need them," she says. "In this society and in this culture, there's a great deal of pain trying to raise men who will become good fathers. It's a growing problem and it's been growing for a long, long time."

"Did your dad encourage your poetic leanings?"

"Yes, he had poetic leanings himself. One of the treasures I inherited at his death was a little notebook he used during military briefings. He took notes, but you would turn the page and find the beginning of a sonnet he was working on."

"Evidence that the briefing got really boring."

"I guess so."

"You once said that you prefer to have poems grow inside you. You said that reading one Rainer Maria Rilke poem can keep you growing for a month, but reading a lot of contemporary poetry is like eating M&Ms. Who are the poets who have made Marilyn Nelson? Who are the poets you keep going back to over the years?"

"Emily Dickinson, Rilke, Robert Hayden, Langston Hughes, Lucille Clifton. There are so many."

"You have a deep affection for kids. How do you encourage their poetic leanings? When they ask you if they're a poet, what do you tell them?"

"I try to dissuade them of any fantasies that they will buy their mother a house with the money they make from their poetry." She laughs. "Then I tell them to enjoy the ride. As an artist, you don't know where your artistry will lead. If it leads to some place that is fulfilling, then be happy. But don't trust it to lead you to fame and fortune—especially poetry. You have to do it for love, not to be published or even read or so your writing will be memorized."

"Love of words and language, of creation?"

"Yes, but mostly the pursuit of truth."

"Do you see your work as inviting readers into a space where you can pursue truth together, where you can commune together? Do you see writing poetry as an act of hospitality?"

"That's a nice image," she says. "I can't say that I've had that picture in my mind while I work, but I like it."

"In your poem 'Cover Photograph,' you wrote that you wanted to be remembered as an 'autumn under maples, a show of incredible leaves.' Life is hard and the road is perilous, so how do we accomplish that?"

"I think it's by looking with the eyes of wonder. It's by looking with a loving gaze. I had a friend, a Catholic priest, who said that when he rode the subway when he was in graduate school, he would pick someone in the subway car to pray for for the duration of the ride. He had this hope that someday, when he entered eternity, some of those people would welcome him in."

"What a gift to give to a stranger. It's an anonymous gift, but it's a gift nonetheless. It takes a great deal of intention to do that."

"Intention yes, but not a lot of effort. You know, you're walking down the street and your eyes catch the eyes of a total stranger and they smile with their eyes and you smile back. That's a gift. It's the gaze of love. You don't have to speak, but you've exchanged something that brightens the human experience. I remember once, when I was a teenager, I was walking across a street. An old white man was crossing toward me. He had two or three dogs on leashes. As we met in the middle of the street, we smiled at each other and he said, 'You are beautiful,' and just kept walking."

"What a rare and wonderful moment, Marilyn. No wonder it has stayed with you all these years."

"Yes, it was such a generous thing to say. I have no idea who that man was or what his life was like, but it was an exchange so powerful that I have remembered it for over sixty years. You know, the blessing that man bestowed on me began with our recognizing our union as human beings. It began with our eyes meeting. So much can change in this world when we look with the gaze of love."

Cover Photograph
by Marilyn Nelson

I want to be remembered
with big bare arms akimbo
and feet splay-toed and flat arched
on the welcome mat of dirt.

I want to be remembered
as a voice that was made to be singing
the lullaby of shadows
as a child fades into a dream.

I want to be as familiar
as the woman in the background
when the heroine is packing
and the Yankee soldiers come.

Hair covered with a bandanna,
I want to be remembered
as an autumn under maples:
a show of incredible leaves.

I want to be remembered
with breasts that never look empty,
with a child-bearing, generous waistline
and with generous, love-making hips.

I want to be remembered
with a dark face absorbing all colors
and giving them back twice as brightly,
like water remembering light.

I want to be remembered
with a simple name, like Mama:
as an open door from creation,
as a picture of someone you know.

ANGELA
ALAIMO
O'DONNELL

"They don't happen a lot. I often think of writing poetry in light of baseball . . . When you're a .300 hitter, that means you're really good. It also means you're missing seven out of ten times at bat. That realization always makes me feel better. Randall Jarrell says that writing poetry is like standing in a parking lot hoping to get struck by lightning, and if it happens seven times in your life, you should count yourself lucky."

—*Angela Alaimo O'Donnell*

I have given the last nearly thirty years of my life to education and, in particular, to the study of literature, so I felt an immediate affinity with Angela Alaimo O'Donnell, who, like me, has given her life to sharing her love with the next generation through teaching. Her passion for Dante and Flannery O'Connor is so deep that she has written a book of poems for each author, but it seemed fitting to start our conversation by thanking her for giving much of her life to teaching the next generation.

"To be a good teacher, you have to give your life away," I say.

"Yes," she says, "there's no doubt it really is a vocation."

"When I read your work and your interviews, you strike me as someone who loves fiercely and with her whole self. Do you love intensely?"

"Absolutely." She laughs and says, "My maiden name, Alaimo, is Sicilian. I love with the ferocity of a Sicilian mother."

"Maybe that's why God gave you three sons."

"Yes. And there's nothing that makes a Sicilian mother happier than having everyone together in the same house. I'm constantly trying to bring them all together. And I suppose that fierce love is a bit of a besetting sin because I'm all in with whatever I'm doing, whether teaching, writing, or parenting. It's a little crazy and obsessive."

"So, you're the kind of person who squeezes 110% out of the 100% of the time, energy, and love God gave her. Is this genetic? Tell me about your parents."

"My father was actually my mother's second marriage. She married a handsome soldier when she was seventeen. Unfortunately, he was unfaithful to her shortly after they married. She got a divorce, which, at the time, was a shameful thing for a Catholic woman. My grandfather did not get an annulment for her, so when she married my father, they had to get married in a civil ceremony, which put her outside of the official church because she was a divorced woman."

"But she remained a practicing Catholic despite the stigma?"

"Yes. She was not going to give up her Catholic identity, so she would dress her five children up on Sunday morning, and we would sit in the front row of the church. She was officially out of communion with the church, but she went anyway. She had a lovely soprano voice, and she would sing louder than everyone else, but when it came time for communion, she wouldn't receive the eucharist. When I was little, I didn't understand. Only when I was older did I realize why she couldn't take communion. Years and years later, after moving to Florida, she called me to say that her first husband had died, which meant that she could now take the sacrament. I never saw my mother take communion until she was in her last days when the priest came to give her last rites."

"Which must have been a moving experience for you."

"Absolutely. And she felt it was very important. She said, 'The priest is coming. He is going to give me holy communion.' It was special to her. By this time, she had reverted to a childlike state. I suppose this happens to all of us when we age. One thing I've learned from time spent with the dying, when you start seeing your mother in the hospital room, you know it means your life journey is coming to a close. I have an unpublished poem about that somewhere in my files. I would have to go digging to find it."

"Is your poetry scattered all over the place when it's in process? Or do you keep it organized?"

"I've developed a system over the years. I keep a journal every day. I write my poems in that journal and mark them with Post-it notes. I revisit them periodically and revise them. I size them up and get a sense for which ones are worth saving and which should never see the light of day. I try to write every day. Of course, not everything I write is going to be a good poem, but you have to keep the muscle active. After some time, I will type up a bunch of the poems that I feel are as good as I can get them. I print them and revise them on paper—adjusting words here and there—and when they're ready, I'll send them out to journals and begin assembling a collection."

"Knowing when something is worthy or unworthy feels a little arbitrary, don't you think?" I ask. "Especially to a young writer. How do you know when something isn't good enough yet?"

"When I was newer to poetry, I was less sure. I was lucky enough to marry a fellow English literature scholar who is a generous and honest reader. I also had fellow poets as friends who would give me feedback. But over time, I have developed my instincts to know when a poem is good or not. For instance, I know that if it doesn't touch me, it won't touch my reader. Some poems just don't pierce through the surface of things in the way I want. So that's one way I decide."

"It still hurts when you have to toss a poem onto the proverbial cutting room floor," I add.

"Yes, but as William Faulkner said, you have to kill your darlings. Some of those poems are about subjects that are very near and dear to my heart, but as poems, they're not as strong as they should be, and they end up diluting the overall experience of my other poems."

"A few years ago," I say, "my editor gave me helpful advice about one of my poems. She told me that I had taken her down a garden path but failed to take her to the very end of the path. She felt like the poem was only half finished." I pause. "To have someone who was not part of the writing process, who didn't know exactly what I was trying to say, but who had the courage and the instinct to offer that kind of feedback was a timely gift," I add.

"That's a great editor. I once had an editor do just the opposite. He said, 'Um, you go on too long. It ends here.' It was already a short poem, but he shortened it even more."

I laugh. "Was he correct?"

"Yes. I mean, I don't remember what he cut because the poem has been in the form he suggested for too many years, but it was a much tighter poem as a result. Sometimes, you need both. Some poems must be shorter. Some should be longer. It takes a wise editor to help with that process. I tend toward compactness, toward shorter poems. I love the sonnet form because I love to work within those limits. The form won't let me go on and on."

"And sometimes there's a risk when a poem is too long, of losing the heat the poem ought to provide."

"Yes. That is a risk, but some poets can write really long poems and maintain the heat. You know, another thing to keep in mind when it comes to writing good poems that keep their heat is that we all get into habits. Even well-regarded poets get into habits of using certain formulaic tricks. You want to avoid making the same moves every time; otherwise, you will lose the heat."

"Don't you think it can be difficult to distinguish between a trick or habit and what might be called a poet's fingerprint, a mark of the poet's style?"

"Yes, that's an important point. That's where readers are helpful. You know, once we release a book into the world, it no longer belongs to us, so readers get to tell us about our own work. They get to tell us about our fingerprints. Sometimes they tell us things that we did not see or did not consciously intend, yet they are valid observations about our work."

"I recently read an article in which the writer said poetry is meant to draw us to attention. I get the picture of a body and heart slumped in the chair of life, only to sit up tall upon reading a poem. But it sounds to me like you write to draw yourself to attention. Maybe that's what resonates with your readers. Because as you draw yourself to attention, they are also drawn to attention."

"You're right. My role as a poet isn't to shake people awake; that's my role as a teacher. With poetry, I attempt to say, 'Hey Self, sit up, pay attention, be alert to what's going on around you.' If I were to describe my mind as a poet, it's like a rabbit, ears raised and twitching, listening. You never know in which direction it might dart. On the other hand, my husband says I'm more like a bird, flitting about, gathering pieces of this or that—ribbon, twig, leaf, seed— to line her nest. I suppose that's what I'm doing with poetry. My material comes from all over the place. Sometimes it comes from the natural world, sometimes from memory, sometimes from popular culture—from a painting or a song I can't stop thinking about. All these disparate experiences are crying out to be ordered in some way. That's what poetry can do. When I don't write, I feel very disordered and de-centered."

"So really, at the end of the day, you write to make

sense of your experience, not to tell people something. That might be the result, but it starts and ends with you."

"Yes. I want to remain myself but also leave myself behind. It's trying to get beyond myself—to open up vistas—while there is also this reflexive move that requires the poet to return to his own life and heart, to ultimately say what it might mean to him and to us."

"Unless that reflexive turn happens, the poem is less likely to have a life of its own," I say, "because it is more like an intellectual exercise than a fully human expression."

"Absolutely. Robert Frost says that poetry is about the relationship between outer and inner weather. So a poet can observe something in the natural world, but he never stays there. What he sees must have some meaning or impact on the inner weather of the perceiver. To simply describe what you see is like a painting by the artist and naturalist John James Audubon. It might be pretty and decorative, but it won't likely move the reader. The poet gives meaning to experience. The return to the self is absolutely necessary if what lies outside the self is to have any impact on the reader and the poet."

"Without necessarily explicating what you see," I add. "Without getting didactic."

"Right," she replies.

"I read a poem yesterday in which the poet was observing nature and said outright that she would impose no meaning on what she saw. For her, it was a virtue simply to observe."

"It always starts with observation," she says, "but I don't think it stays there."

"I can understand where she's coming from," I say. "We shouldn't impose our own meaning on things, but because God made all things and because he holds all things together, even what appears meaningless has meaning woven into it. The meaning just isn't always obvious."

"I don't think a poet should impose meaning on experience, but I do think meaning still emerges. As humans, we constantly look for meaning. Sometimes, a poet needs to provide the image and allow the reader to find the meaning. I recently read a poem about a bird trying to get a twig that was too large into its little birdhouse. Just presenting the image was enough."

"Yes, it opens onto various meanings for the reader."

"Right, but the poet insisted on adding a stanza in which she unpacked the meaning for us. It wasn't necessary. It was didactic. That's a teacher's job, not a poet's."

"This conversation reminds me of the psalmist who spends much of his time talking to himself," I say. "He's looking for meaning; he's finding meaning, but not just any meaning. He's trying to see how God sees. The meaning is emerging, but he's making sure it has a semblance of truth."

"One of the hallmarks of the Catholic imagination is to recognize that everything means something and it means it intensely," she says. "As Gerard Manley Hopkins put it, 'The world is charged with the grandeur of God.' Creation, every single thing, points back to its maker. In that respect, every created thing is a living thing, alive with the fire God put into it. One of the poet's jobs is to note that fire and to help us see it. I think God has even given this gift to unbelieving poets; he lets them see a glimpse of that fire and wonder in nature and the human heart. The best poets, regardless of religious beliefs, have this sense that there's something greater than us, something transcendent that everything points toward. Robert Frost was not a terribly religious man, but there's no question that as a poet he saw these things around him and, therefore, made them visible to us as well."

"Don't you find that the great poets have a hunger for something beyond themselves, that they keep pointing at that something even though they may not know what to call it?" I ask.

"Yes, something greater than us, something greater than our understanding. Even the best scientists have this sense of things beyond our ken. The language they use might be the language of mathematics, but there is ultimately a sense of mystery. The best scientists are not materialists. You need a great imagination to be a great scientist. Actually, you need a great imagination to be a great human being, because there's something inside us that cries out, that longs to elucidate the wonder at the heart of all things, at the heart of our deepest selves, so that others can see it. We long to see things in light of eternity, to see meaning that is not time-bound."

"You're talking about the full gamut of human experience, which includes a great deal of hurt. So, even in our suffering, we long to find meaning. And we want to elucidate that meaning somehow. In your book *Still Pilgrim*, you say of your younger self that 'she knew herself lonely, didn't belong with the happy kids.' Although you strike me as someone whose joy bubbles over, there's much hurt in your life. It seems to me that the woman you are today has grown up with her roots in the soil of sadness. Would you say that you are straining light through poetry?"

"Absolutely. Writing helps. It's not an accident that soldiers who return from war are given writing classes. It gives them an opportunity to articulate the trauma of what they have experienced. Writing is an important part of healing. We should do more of it. I started young, maybe five or six. There was a part of me that really wanted to become an opera singer, but we couldn't afford singing lessons, so that was out. But I could write poems. All I needed was a piece of paper, a pen, and a love for words. I discovered that there was something powerful about recording the things that happened to me. Those events became more meaningful and consequential, making poetry made me feel like I mattered more. It was a tremendously empowering experience. More importantly, the poems redeemed the poverty, alienation, and darkness I experienced."

"Redeemed, I'm assuming, not simply by the retelling, but by how you lit the experience? I'm thinking of Rembrandt and the way he would light his subjects, impoverished or ugly as they might be."

"Yes. In some ways poets are myth-makers, making intentional decisions about how certain events will be remembered without lying about the events. We're imposing order on events by the choices we make, the way we use language, poetic forms, and all the tools at our disposal. And that's important for the human experience. Many of the greatest poems were born out of suffering, from an urge to make some kind of sense of it, to create an order that will redeem the suffering."

"So it matters very much how we light the subject, whether the subject is grievous or whether it is joyous."

"I like to think of Saint Ignatius, who illuminates the full gamut of human experience. There are poems of desolation and poems of consolation. Or Hopkins, with his sonnets of joy and the so-called 'Terrible Sonnets,' chronicling a soul that is suffering and feeling a sense of loss and distance from God. We should write those kinds of poems and every kind in between. God not only permits us to do so but calls us to do so."

"And the psalmists lead in that example. You're reminding me of a line by Seamus Heaney: 'I rhyme to see myself, to set the darkness echoing.'"

"I love that poem, 'Personal Helicon,' because it depicts a child kneeling at the edge of the well to see what he can see down in the depths. He can't see much, and what he can see is scary—a rat that slaps across the water—yet he keeps looking. That's when he realizes that although he can't understand everything, he can make songs that set the darkness echoing."

"Which comes as a surprise."

"A surprise and a gift. The poem becomes a surprise, and even moments in the poem can surprise the one writing it. As Frost says, if there's no surprise in the writer, there's no surprise in the reader. This happened to me with a poem called 'The Still Pilgrim Honors Her Mother.' When I was a little girl, I used to watch my mother get dressed. It was a complicated ritual in those days, so this sonnet is fairly straightforward until the final three lines, which went in a direction I didn't expect. The poem ends this way:

> *Her narrow waist encased in folds of flesh,*
> *Five pregnancies leaving their mark.*
> *In a world of rain, she was our ark.*

"As often happens when I write in form, I had no idea what the poem's final line would be. I wrote the second to last line knowing that I would need a couplet to complete this sonnet, and there aren't that many words that rhyme with 'mark.' Just like that, the word 'ark' struck me with tremendous force. Suddenly, and without my engineering it, I knew what my mother had been for us. With my father dying when I was young, with all of the sorrow and poverty, she was an ark."

"That's a beautiful story. I assume those kinds of grace moments don't happen with every poem, but when they do, they're startling."

"Exactly. You're right. They don't happen a lot. I often think of writing poetry in light of baseball. My husband and my three sons love the game, and we watch a lot of baseball. When you're a .300 hitter, that means you're really good. It also means you're missing seven out of ten times at bat. That realization always makes me feel better. Randall Jarrell says that writing poetry is like standing in a parking lot hoping to get struck by lightning, and if it happens seven times in your life, you should count yourself lucky."

"That's really funny," I say. "I've never heard that before."

"Kind of a frightening thought, but pretty spot-on."

"Can we talk about form poetry?"

"Sure."

"In a recent article, Abram Van Engen mentioned that the word 'stanza' comes from the Italian for 'little room.' That seems to be an apt description of your work. Each stanza plays host to the reader, welcoming us into not merely an idea or a statement but a place where we are changed. Do you see yourself as creating little rooms? Are you decorating and furnishing them as an act of hospitality? Are you creating beautiful spaces for readers to enter and commune with you?"

"I love that image! As you know, among the Greeks

and Mediterraneans, hospitality is the highest virtue. The person you turn away at the door could be one of the gods. And from the book of Hebrews, how do you know but that you might be entertaining angels unawares? My whole family is obsessed with hospitality. To be inhospitable is the worst sin imaginable. Dante doesn't include the inhospitable circles of hell, which is problematic for me—it's a major oversight. Am I allowed to say that of the great Dante?"

"That's funny. Yes, you can say it, but I'll only let you say it this one time."

"Thank you. So I love this idea. Yes, each poem issues an invitation to enter the poet's world, to see what she sees, to be together in this moment. They don't have to be large and ornate rooms; they can be small and simple. I would go so far as to say that each line is its own little room opening onto other rooms. I love those lines from Emily Dickinson: "I dwell in Possibility – / a fairer House than Prose – / More numerous of Windows – / Superior – for Doors –." I love the idea that a poem has multiple doors and windows by which the reader might enter. So, in my poem about my mother, the word 'ark' invites you into the poem even though it comes at the end. It calls you to read the poem again, but with new eyes. I think form is essential. You're not very hospitable when you just cast a bunch of syllables onto the page in a chaotic fashion. Anyone can toss words onto the page, but it takes hard work to build something beautiful."

"When I was in high school, poems struck me as random acts; a poem was a riddle. They made me miserable. Even the poems written in form felt like riddles, which were fun to untangle for those who liked riddles, but they still weren't very inviting. It seemed to me that poets were writing something out of reach just to show they could do it. I wasn't even sure they knew what they were talking about."

"Yes, that can be frustrating."

"Over the years, I've decided that there's a distinction between poets who abandon form entirely for the sake of being obtuse and those who still hold to musicality without necessarily using formal structures."

"That's helpful. I also think some poets are more oral, and some are more visual. Maybe that accounts for some of the differences. Some poets like to write in open form, to see the poem on the page, and to pay attention to the relationship between each line and the negative space around it. For others, it's all about the images and the sounds. I'm very much an ear-centric poet, but I greatly respect those poets who can write free verse well. My tastes are eclectic. I have a deep appreciation for a varied array of poetry styles. Part of why I respect those poets is that I find it very difficult to write free verse. Over the years, I've learned to go with my predilections."

"Yes," I say. "Though these differences can create unhealthy rivalry among poets. We live in a society of envy. We and our children are catechized in the doctrines of desires that ultimately destroy us and our relationships."

"Dante treats envy in a unique and powerful way in *Purgatorio*. The envious are punished by having their eyes sutured shut. The punishment excites Dante's compassion because he can understand the temptation. It's human nature to be quickened by desire for what we do not have. As I say in one of my 'Dear Dante' poems, it seems easy, if you're blind, to avoid the temptation of envy, so in some respects, the person with his eyes sewn shut is blessed. We live in a culture saturated by images; we're constantly presented with beautiful, desirable things. It's hard not to want them."

"It's not just on television or billboards anymore; it's wherever I go on the internet and social media," I say.

"That's right. It's hard to be a human being amid all that gorgeous plenty. My students have said that they have to get off social media because they feel worthless when they watch the exciting lives of their so-called friends play out. I mean, let's be honest, there's nothing more curated, more artificial, than what we put on social media, and that's part of what sets us up for envy. It devalues the normality of our day-to-day lives."

"Social media is a different kind of myth-making."

"Definitely," she replies.

"Saint Augustine understood this when he wrote in *City of God* that our desires are the seat of our actions and they need proper ordering if we were to live good lives."

"Yes," she replies. "I have all sorts of disordered desires. My relationship to the Amazon man alone says it all. I love the Amazon guy because he always brings me something wonderful. It will make me happy! Then, of course, the shine wears off, and I need something else. Dante would say that I'm in Amazon purgatory."

"Ha! Well, I assure you, you're not alone."

"I decided it was worth writing a poem about that problem as a way to help me wrestle with my disordered desire. Poetry and the act of writing poetry is a way of combating the false myth-making around us and that we ourselves engage in, pointing the heart to what is beautiful, good, and true in hopes that the poem may help others along the way. First and foremost, it helps me focus on what I should focus on. It has been that way for many years, and it will remain that way as long as I write."

The Still Pilgrim Hosts Christ,
by Angela Alaimo O'Donnell

Christ came calling one Christmas Day.
He brought us birds and scoops of sky.
His bag filled with fruit and buckets of rain.
His backpack humming with hives of bees.
We'd never need honey or bread again,
or fish or olives or homemade cheese.
He set them all out on a table he brought
and bid us all sit down and eat.

None of us wondered. All of us thought
How nice of Christ! and claimed a seat.
He smiled as we tasted each sweet meat.
He told us stories, and, God, he could sing.
He was the best guest Christmas could bring.
He stayed until dark, then left everything.

TANIA RUNYAN

"I think poetry helps us be more human, less artificial. There's so much gamesmanship and posturing on social media. There's so much fear. Reading and writing poetry allows you to explore one's own soul or feelings without fear. Works of art can cut through all of the meanness in the world, all of the artificiality, and touch us deeply. We need to recover what it means to be really human."

—*Tania Runyan*

Tania Runyan is one of those rare gems whose laughter and energy are contagious. Her prolific pen and thousand activities are due as much to her dogged determination as to her many loves. Of course, a family will keep one busy, too. That's why I decided to rope them into my opening foray of questions.

"How would your kids and husband describe Tania Runyan?"

"I'm so glad you sent your question beforehand so I could ask my family," she says. "Otherwise, I would have no idea. Is that cheating?"

"Yes." I laugh. "What did they say?"

"They were very sweet about it. Here's their list. They said I was loving, generous, wise, fun, caring, determined, hardworking, comforting, funny, courageous, and patient."

"Sheesh! Pretty much the perfect human being. You should give them a raise in their allowance."

"I really should."

"Did they elaborate on their answers?"

"No, of course not."

"You have said that you're an introvert with people skills. That you love people, but that you need to reboot in solitude."

"Yes, I guess I'm fairly decent at starting conversations, building community in a classroom, drawing out the best in people, and making people feel loved. But I know that I am an introvert because all of that 'peopling' comes at a cost. If I don't provide myself with large swaths of solitary time to balance out interactions, I become drained and even a bit depressed. This is why I have never been able to sustain teaching for very long. I adore students and make good connections with them, but my energy cannot keep up with my heart. I am at my best when I work and write alone, interspersed with opportunities to speak, teach, and connect before burrowing back into my cave under my pile of dogs."

"I'm glad to spend some time with a fellow introvert and dog lover," I say. "This might be an overgeneralization, but it seems to me that many poets are introverts. What makes introverts uniquely equipped to write poetry?"

"It's the solitude, really. I don't think it's about being shy or more thoughtful or anything like that. Because we love solitude and need solitude, we have the opportunity to write. It's hard to write when there are a lot of people around. It's not even about the quiet so much as the opportunity to be alone. I can't get enough solitude. I need it a lot, but I also love people a lot, so it's tough. I'm torn."

"I wonder if solitude predisposes the heart to reflection in a way that crowds simply cannot."

"I don't know. I can be in the presence of people and still reflect and think about things. A huge factor is whether I'm stressed by the company and whether I'm responsible for them or not. That puts a strain on me."

"Have you been this way since you were a kid?" I ask.

"Yes, actually. I was a latchkey kid. My older sister is fourteen years older than me; I was raised like an only child. I had so much time to myself that I had to find ways to entertain myself. One of those ways was reading. Believe it or not, I loved reading encyclopedias, atlases, *Peanuts* cartoons, and comic books. I read novels, too, but that wasn't my main diet back then. I became very comfortable with solitude, but it was still a language-rich childhood."

"Someone once said that solitude is the home of

the strong and silence is their prayer. Do you resonate with that?"

"I would have to think about it. I suppose, to some degree, it does. But I'm not a very quiet person. For instance, I'm always listening to music. You know, some people hear the word 'solitude' and they, I don't know . . ."

"They imagine a monastic life?"

"Yes, and that's nothing like the life I live. I just like being alone."

"You can pick your own music, for goodness sake!"

We laugh. "Yes, exactly," she says.

"There are some poets I read whose poetry feels like it was born out of silence. Other poets don't give me that sense. I don't know how to explain it."

"Can you give me an example?"

"Well, I feel that way when I read the poetry of Li-Young Lee."

"He's amazing," she says.

"Do you get the same sense?"

"I think I know what you're talking about. But you're right; it's hard to explain."

"I don't feel that way about your poetry," I say. "That's not an insult; it's just an uncanny sense. Your poetry feels different somehow, more vigorous in some respects."

"Some people have said that my poetry is raw and gritty. I'm not purposefully trying to be raw or gritty; it's just my way of looking the subject in the eye. But to your point, I'm not contemplative or silent in my bearing. I'm active. I like to do things."

"*Library Journal* called you acerbic."

She laughs. "Well, that one makes a lot of sense to me. I mean, sarcasm is one of my love languages. Teasing is proof of relational love. It's proof that I feel comfortable around you."

"When did you start experimenting with writing?"

"A babysitter got me into writing when I was around seven, challenging me to make a story about one of her animal posters. I created a cast of funny talking animals who lived in an apartment together—think *Three's Company.* I will never forget the sensation of reading something that I created. I didn't want to stop! But I wasn't the traditional literary kid who read *The Secret Garden*, *A Wrinkle in Time*, and so forth. Because I watched a lot of TV, I was very tuned to the rhythms of dialogue and would write scripts, playing different parts I would speak into my portable tape recorder. I dreamed of becoming a screenwriter."

"Did you write any novels?"

"I didn't have the attention span for that, but I did

start collecting pen pals. At one point, I had over fifty. This was when I was twelve to fifteen."

"Oh my goodness!"

"I know. I had some in other countries, but most lived in different parts of the United States. They fascinated me. I was very curious about their lives. I would get one or two letters a day. This was back in the day when your mailbox was a mail flap in the front door, so the mail just dropped onto your floor. It was so rewarding! I would be by myself, and then I would hear the mail flap and there would be letters. I'd reply right away because I loved the human connection made through language. I've loved that connection ever since."

"So writing poetry came later in life."

"It wasn't until my senior year of high school that a creative writing teacher told me she thought I was really a poet at heart. I finally accepted that a few years into college and changed my emphasis from playwriting to poetry."

"Is writing poetry a way for you to explore life and untangle your thoughts?" I ask.

"Absolutely. I never write to teach anything or to express a truth. I write for myself. I write to figure things out. Even when I wrote *Second Sky*, about the Apostle Paul and his writings, or *What Will Soon Take Place*, about the book of Revelation, I was trying to grapple with those things, not to teach people about what I've learned."

"When you say that it's a way to figure things out, you're not talking about solving things or writing tidy poetry that puts a bow on your thoughts," I suggest. "At least, I don't think you are, because your poetry is very open-ended."

"Good, I'm glad to hear that," she says.

"How do you reconcile open-endedness and 'figuring things out'?"

"I guess when I say that I'm figuring things out," she replies, "I'm not saying that I'm finding an answer. I'm sitting with it, engaging the subject honestly and allowing a sense of mystery to remain. That doesn't mean that I forsake the craft of writing poetry. I don't believe in emoting on the page or brain-dumping in hopes that my readers will discover something transcendent in my chaos. But at the same time, I'm not looking for a tidy bow to put on my experience."

"In the book *Hard Times*, by Dickens," I say, "there's a girl named Sissy Jupe who has grown up around horses because her father is a horse trainer, but she can't give an adequate definition of a horse. Mr. Gradgrind rebukes her and calls on one of the boys in the class to help her.

The boy's definition is correct, but only technically. The cruel irony is that Sissy is the only one in the room who really knows what a horse actually is. She has a more experiential, poetic knowledge. Bookish knowledge and poetic knowledge are valuable, but one is two-dimensional and the other is three-dimensional. Poetic knowledge is richer, born out of intimacy with horses."

"I couldn't say it better than that. Yes, that's exactly it. I'm writing as an act of exploring in the hopes of gaining intimate, poetic knowledge of what I'm exploring. Whether it's characters in the Bible, everyday events, or people."

"I had a young person ask me once, 'What is poetry for?' How would you answer that?"

"My goodness, that's a difficult question. How did *you* answer her?"

I grin and shake my head. "I thought I was the one asking the questions here," I reply.

"You are," she says, "I'm just curious."

"Okay, the honest answer is that I didn't have a ready response, so I asked her what the psalms are for. It probably wasn't playing fair, but it got us started."

"What did she say?"

"Well, the question made her pause—which bought me time to think—and it made her realize that there isn't a quick answer to the question," I say. "The psalms are too complex and too beautiful. They're so meaningful, they resist reduction. The psalmists give us words to articulate what we wouldn't know how to articulate, they explore the full gamut of human experience in beautiful language that reflects the surging in the human heart. The psalms give us language to talk to ourselves and to God. We also find comfort and encouragement in the psalms, but those come from relating to the psalmists, not necessarily from getting more information."

"That's really good," she says.

"Well, it was a fun discussion, but it was a long discussion, because the question can't be answered concisely. It struck me later that the question presupposes a practical end. It starts by assuming everything has to be good for something, that a piece of art can't just exist for the sake of existing or for the sake of adding something beautiful to the world. Beauty doesn't bow to our pragmatism. Music doesn't either. Neither does poetry."

"I think poetry helps us drill down into what it means to be human. It gets to the heart of being a person."

"I was just reading *Braided Creek*, an exchange of short poems between Ted Kooser and Jim Harrison. It's a wonderful collection. In the forward, Naomi Shihab Nye comments on how the poems startle her in new ways each time she reads the book. She asks whether the poems have changed, somehow, in the time since her earlier reading, or if she has changed. Do you have that experience?"

"Yes, certainly, with the best poems. I find that it's true with poems by Li-Young Lee and others. You know, the first time I encountered his work was in college. My best friend took me to Barnes and Noble—or maybe it was Borders. I had never seen such a thing. So many books! We found the poetry section. I was astounded that there was such a thing as a poetry section, because I thought poetry only came from anthologies and textbooks. Without much rhyme or reason, I bought three books: Li-Young Lee's *Rose*, Mary Oliver's *American Primitive*, and *Gold Cell* by Sharon Olds. I remember the sheer wonder and charm of holding those books and then reading such approachable poems in them."

"Those poets write about everyday things," I say.

"Exactly. And I didn't have to fight through the language to understand what they were saying. In graduate school, when I was getting my MFA, there were some poets that I just couldn't understand. I had so much trouble getting through the language that I felt, I don't know, a sense of imposter syndrome—like I was a fraud who didn't belong in this world of poetry. I would tell my professor, 'I don't know what I am reading.' It didn't help that she told me, 'Some people's brains just don't work that way.' Not very comforting. The abstractions were so alienating. But those three poets were so concrete, so sensory. The *who*, *what*, and *where* of the poems were clear, so I could enter the poem and get my footing. When those things are clear, I can take my time with the *why*."

"One poet I talked to distinguished between ambiguity and mystery. She said the former was connected to confusion and the latter was tied to not knowing. She said that some poets relish confusion and ambiguity, confusing them for mystery."

"Exactly," she says. "Those poets were concrete and clear, so I could be enchanted by the *why* as it dawned on me. And they earned my trust by being clear, so I was willing to follow them into mystery. The poets I encountered in that store wrote about regular things— parenting and pregnancy and nature. Now, after living into my fifties, I have more experience with those things, so the poems strike me differently than they did when I was in my twenties. At the time, they sounded beautiful in the mouth, but now their meaning has deepened. The poems are the same, but I have changed. For all that, they haven't lost their potency and charm. In some ways, it has increased with age."

"When I read your poems, I'm struck by how hard you work to honor your subject. None of your poems feel casual or flippant."

"I'm glad to hear that. I know that sometimes people are a little surprised when they meet me to find out that I'm so goofy and that I laugh so much, because my poems are so serious and sometimes violent. I even have a few curse words in them, but I never swear in real life. I don't like violent movies. It's kind of funny. I'm not a serious intellectual. I don't sit there in candlelight while I write. I love colorful clothing and flowers. And I love to laugh."

"Alfred, Lord Tennyson was known for his laughter. People loved to be around him. The older he got the more he laughed, even though his poems were increasingly about human depravity, failure, and loss. I wonder if the ability to look the ugliness in the eye freed him. He writes with such care and tenderness, so it's not a flippant laughter. He just enjoyed life."

"When I wrote *A Thousand Vessels*, I tried to write about biblical women with great care and love, so hopefully that comes through. They were regular women, just like me, so I tried to write about regular, everyday things. I don't have a choice. I live in the suburbs. I drive a minivan."

"It's the material you have to work with."

"Yes, I'm writing out of the reality of my life."

"There's a poem in that collection called 'My Daughter's Hands.' In it, you describe the communion tray passing and the way your daughter tried to grab the cup. The line that caught my attention was, 'Yet I know the moment I say *no* / your world will begin to go wrong.' In our church, communion is a weekly thing and I love that. I love that my children and I get to partake of the sacrament together. I think it's an important yes that they are invited to the table with me. It's a yes that shapes them. Of course, being a parent requires that I say *no* to them often if I'm going to help them order their desires, but this is not one of those moments. I know that I'm on debatable ground here, but it seems to me that when we deny them access to the table, we're saying something about their Father in Heaven."

"Absolutely," she says.

"I also know that my kids imitate me, so I want them to see me reaching for the cup of blessing rather than, say, reaching for my cell phone. I want them to see me communing with Christ, not communing with social media. As they navigate this life, I want them to return to the foundation of the sacraments."

"Well, that little girl is now twenty-one years old, so a lot of life has happened. When I wrote those early poems, I had no idea what my kids would face in the world. My daughter, like everyone in her generation, has been shaped by things I never imagined possible. Massive forces are working on this generation. Obviously, I can't change the fact that there was a pandemic, and I can't change the fact that social media is rewiring the brain chemistry of a whole generation of humans. I wish I could. And politics, too. When we were kids, politics mattered, but the political climate was not nearly what it is today. It's heartbreaking what this generation has gone through."

"I agree."

"They're growing up in a world that is so politically charged that nearly everything in their life is colored by conflict. They are being wired—we're being wired—to think in terms of conflict first."

"You can't have a normal conversation about a minor disagreement," I say, "because it's just too much, it's overwhelming."

"Yes. Unless it's about nothing at all, every conversation is supercharged, and we become more silent or tiptoe through a field of landmines. And the phone's impact on their lives is massive. They have to navigate so much that's right at their fingertips."

"When we were young, kids had to go looking for pornography. Now it comes to find them."

"That's so true. It's a horrible, horrible situation."

"How does poetry help?" I ask.

"I think poetry helps us be more human, less artificial. There's so much gamesmanship and posturing on social media. There's so much fear. Reading and writing poetry allows you to explore your own soul or feelings without fear. Works of art can cut through all of the meanness in the world, all of the artificiality, and touch us deeply. We need to recover what it means to be human."

"I think it was C. S. Lewis who said that we read to know that we're not alone. That's also partly why people use social media. But there must be a difference between social media affirmation and poetry affirmation."

"Yes, poetry offers a deeper affirmation of our shared humanity. I use social media. I like using it. There's an instant gratification to it. The response is almost immediate. Connection happens quickly. It's not a far cry from my pen pals earlier in life. But if I could go back and get rid of social media, I would do it. I'm not sure where I read this, but there was an article that covered some fascinating findings from a survey of young people. When they were asked if they would prefer a world with social media or without social media, their overwhelming response was that if everyone dropped social media at the same time, they would be fine with it. They would even be willing to pay for that to happen. But if anyone still had it and they didn't, they would want to keep social media. Fear of missing out was that strong in them. Even though they know it's taking their joy away, they still fear being left out."

"That's an incredible finding."

"Our lives are shaped and run by social media, but we don't really want it that way. Even kids know that they are more human when they don't have their phone and they have no access to social media. It's a crushing realization that knowing the truth doesn't compel us to do anything about it."

"Poetry slows us down," I add. "I find that social media speeds me up inside, but poetry doesn't do that."

"I agree."

"I wonder how much of that slowing down has to do with gratitude. Social media doesn't help me be more grateful. It doesn't always make me more envious, of course, but it doesn't make me content. I wonder if reading poetry can help us become more grateful. There are many poets whose roots are in the soil of gratitude and it is evident in their poetry. "

"Absolutely. Li-Young Lee and Mary Oliver certainly belong to that group. I think it's an important daily task to write down things I'm grateful for. Maybe it's only coffee and birdsong, but I'm still taking a moment to pause. Poetry gives me the chance to live into my senses, to be more aware and, therefore, more thankful," she says. "The act of writing, for me, is a way of staying connected to Christ. That, alone, is a worthy purpose for picking up the pen."

Mary at the Nativity
by Tania Runyan

The angel said there would be no end
to his kingdom. So for three hundred days
I carried rivers and cedars and mountains.
Stars spilled in my belly when he turned.

Now I can't stop touching his hands,
the pink pebbles of his knuckles,
the soft wrinkle of flesh
between his forefinger and thumb.
I rub his fingernails as we drift
in and out of sleep. They are small
and smooth, like almond petals.
Forever, I will need nothing but these.

But all night, the visitors crowd
around us. I press his palms to my lips
in silence. They look down in anticipation,
as if they expect him to suddenly
spill coins from his hands
or raise a gold scepter
and turn swine into angels.

Isn't this wonder enough
that yesterday he was inside me,
and now he nuzzles next to my heart?
That he wraps his hand around
my finger and holds on?

LUCI
SHAW

"It's not easy to be a poet because much of our society sees poetry as extraneous, an add-on that's not vital. But poetry is vital. It offers us meaningful words, deep words to overcome the meaningless chatter all around us."

—*Luci Shaw*

At ninety-five, Luci Shaw may have difficulty with mobility, but her mind and heart are as strong as ever—proof of which is her new book of poetry, *Reversing Entropy*. I first encountered Luci Shaw through one of her essays. Her writing was insightful, yet personable and kind, preoccupied with seeing everything through God's eyes. At the time, I remember thinking that if I ever became a writer, I would very much like to sound like her, to see like her.

At the start of our conversation, I thank her for teaching me the value of the sanctified imagination.

"Well, imagination is a gift," she says. "It is something that can be grown in a good or a bad direction, so I think we have to treat this gift like all of God's other gifts. We must give it back to God."

"How would you say that poetry speaks uniquely to the imagination?" I ask.

"Poetry is different from mere history or fiction. Poetry calls for a different response from the reader. It asks a reader to enter a room with the poet—beyond facts and information—to a realm of image-making in our heads. Imagination is making pictures in our minds and allowing God to use that capacity to create new things, new ideas into the world. That comes from reading and listening. I try to read good writing as a way to inform my imagination. Putting words onto paper takes a certain journey of the mind because you see something in your head and somehow you have to put it into a form that is accessible to the reader. Being familiar with good language and good poets makes all the difference to the quality of one's work."

"What poets do you return to again and again to inform your imagination, to inspire you?" I ask.

"There are some wonderful contemporary poets in the Christian tradition," she says. "Scott Cairns is one. Paul Mariani is another. They write searching poetry and prose that leads the reader to a new realization. That's how I want to go about my work, too. I love it when an image or a metaphor is provided to me and I can take that and follow it to a new arena of understanding."

"You've shared before that poetry has always been a part of your life. Was that because poetry served as a comfort to you? Was it a way to process life experience from an early age?"

"My father was a lover of poetry. He did not write poetry himself, but he read the romantics—William Wordsworth and Samuel Coleridge and the like. I remember him reading them aloud to me. The way the language fashioned images in my head was formative to my own imagination. I began writing poems when I was six or seven years old. I didn't realize it was anything special. I would write them on small pieces of paper and give them to my dad. He would show them to his friends. He was just so proud of his daughter and that was a great encouragement to me." She laughs, recalling her father.

"One of the great gifts my dad gave his kids was that he put us in really good schools, private schools, which took a great deal of money. But it was worth it because they had the kind of quality and expectation that called forth good work from students. The other thing that really affected me was that my dad was a conference speaker. We lived in Australia, Canada, and the United States, so we were exposed to many cultures. Australia was especially formative to me. I remember going out to the mountains, smelling the eucalyptus, letting it fill my lungs. The great sandy beaches around Sydney. It was a rich childhood and the fact that I was in a good school and I had good teachers made all the difference in the world."

"The world needs more fathers like yours. It sounds like he invested in you in multiple ways. Not just financial support, but emotional support, which played a major role in your hope for the future. I love the simple picture of your dad sharing his loves with you."

"Yes, indeed." She pauses. "And, you know, in particular reading aloud to us. We didn't have a lot of children's books. Maybe *Winnie-the-Pooh*, but not much more to call on. But we loved to hear words read aloud. My parents would read really good adult fiction to me. That's how I learned how words worked. Hearing good literature imprints itself somehow on the mind with an unexplainable quality. But, you know, I was also shaped by learning different languages. I studied Latin, French, and I had a minor in New Testament Greek. I think learning a language can be such an enriching experience. Words, you know."

"You're touching on an important point here," I say. "Something that recalls to mind several lines from Naomi Shihab Nye. She writes, "Words— / otherwise it is just a world with a lot of rough edges, / difficult to get through, and our pockets full of / stones." Is that what you are talking about?

"Yes, but more. In the beginning was the Word, you know, and we were made to be in relationship with that

Word, allowing it to seep into our own lives so that we can speak what is true and beautiful."

"It sounds to me like you're saying it's not just the words under the words," I say, "but the Word under the words that is most meaningful to you."

"Yes, indeed."

"What would you say are the stones in our pockets that are weighing us down these days, and how does poetry minister to people burdened by such stones?"

"That is a very potent question. In this life of ours, where politics has taken such a huge part of our thinking and our understanding, I find it stretching my soul with anger and frustration. Politics seems to take the worst of human motivation and human action and turn it sour. It just eats at my soul. But at my church, there's such an emphasis on God's word, the words of Scripture. So I get good food in that way. We have to choose whether we will listen to Scripture or to the ugly words of political strife."

"Has all of this taken a toll on your poetry?" I ask.

"You know, I've been very fortunate to have had two different husbands over the years who have given me the freedom to write poetry, to get away and work on my craft despite whatever is calling for my attention. It's not easy to be a poet because much of our society sees poetry as extraneous, an add-on that's not vital. But poetry is vital. It offers us meaningful words, deep words to overcome the meaningless chatter all around us."

"How has community played a role in your career?"

"I belong to this wonderful group of people called The Chrysostom Society. Richard Foster, Madeleine L'Engle, and I decided that we wanted to pull together some of our friends who were writers to hear each other read and speak and then to develop books from those gatherings. I think my friendship with Madeleine was another true gift to me. For thirty-five years, we were each other's best friend. She came from the far left, from the liberal side of the church, and I came from the far right, and we met somewhere in the middle. God was so rich in our understanding of life and of truth. That was one of the gifts God gave to me. I miss her terribly." She pauses.

Then, as though renewed by memory, she says, "We both lost our first husbands to cancer in the same year, you know. She was traveling in the middle of the Atlantic when she had a terrible feeling that something had happened to my husband, Harold, and that it was bad. When she landed, she called me right away to discover that he had died. You know, somehow that connection was made. We don't understand it, but it is evidence of our closeness."

"You and L'Engle share a similar spirit in your writing," I say. "Did you share a similar hope for what you might have accomplished by the time your life comes to a close?"

"Yes, I think you just keep trying to take the picture in your head and do your best to communicate with words what that picture is. I have a book of poetry coming out with Paraclete Press in a few weeks called *Reversing Entropy*. I'm just hoping I'll still be alive so I can see the book and promote it for them. I look forward to reading the words aloud from the page. Poetry has a special entry to the mind because it has a musicality to it."

"I'm just amazed that God has given you such strength of heart and mind at the age of ninety-five," I say. "When you look back over your work, do you feel as though each previous book was a kind of rehearsal for the next one?"

"That's a wonderful way of looking at it," she replies. "I suppose so. Each book is further along in your life and, hopefully, more true to the medium you are writing in. I hope to be always growing as a writer. I never feel like I've got it figured out. Poetry is a kind of grace, both gentle and strong. It should sharpen our experience of nature, of relationship, and the world around us. I'm so thankful that I live in a part of the world that has such natural beauty. We live in a house on a hill and can look out our living room windows at Washington's Bellingham Bay and the islands beyond it. We have Mount Baker within an hour of us. We love to drive up that huge mountain and see our part of the world."

"The Pacific Northwest is, indeed, a beautiful part of the world."

"You know, I think nature gives us clues as to what ultimately matters and what is ultimately beautiful, you know. I don't know how many years I have to live, but I hope I can live through a couple more cycles of seasons just because they are so rich. They speak to me. I'm an amateur photographer. I have a little camera that allows me to capture beauty. My husband drives me slowly through the woods around here and I'll say to him, 'Stop, stop here. I just saw something I want to photograph.' The buttercups, the cowslips, it's all so available to us. I don't think we appreciate the availability of beauty to us. Life is more than the job we do, more than providing food for your family. You know, I love writing poetry and I'm thankful to bookstores that sell my books, but you don't make a lot of money from writing poetry. It provides food for the mind, but not much food for the dining room table.

It's about feeding the soul and I think nature does that well, direct from the hand of God."

"You're reminding me of the poem 'How To Be a Poet,' by Wendell Berry. He writes, 'Accept what comes from silence. Make the best you can of it.' And 'make a poem that does not disturb the silence from which it came.' It sounds like you find that silence in nature."

"I certainly do. I love Wendell Berry. I have a wonderful collection of his poetry."

"You've received a lot of praise for your work over the years," I say. "How has that affected your writing? I'm thinking here of young poets who want approval, who need some encouragement along the way. How have you made sure that the praise does not warp the way you write your poems?"

"Friendships with kindred spirits are vital," she replies. "I have a group of friends that meet together every week. We talk about God and about each other. Each person is so unique and yet we can share what we have in common. The Chrysostom Society, too. All this richness provides perspective."

"My final question isn't really a question, but I'm curious how you would complete the following, 'Dear Poet…'"

"I would say, never give up on the grace of God. And keep meeting together with kindred spirits to push forward imaginative work."

Green, Springing
by Luci Shaw

Down the hill, over the river,
beside the dirt track I walk slowly
enough to stop, to listen for the pale
whisper of increment floating from
the tassels, the maiden buds,
the nascent leaves lifting their heads
—little green flames, more
chartreuse than emerald.

Now I hear it clearly. They are
telling their way into being
and calling us to join in.
The air is full of green pilgrims who
walk together in this God-light.

It is the best season. There is
such courage in bursting life.
And yes, I promise, it is possible—
to fulfill God's reason for thrusting us
into full leaf, rooted in our
unique, particular ground.

RYAN
WHITAKER
SMITH

"There are phrases from those writers [John Donne and George Herbert] that have never left me. It still amazes me that you can read those guys even today and be moved in our day and age without strobe lights or smoke machines. It's just words on a page, but tears come to my eyes. Those guys never set out to be culture makers, to be famous. They were just trying to be honest with God."

—Ryan Whitaker Smith

We met in a coffee shop that my teenagers would have considered bougie. Is that the word? At any rate, my dad would have called it swanky. Sitting there, you could imagine a wealthy old woman dressed in fur carrying her fluffy little dog up to the barista for a doggie drink. I didn't have to imagine it. That actually happened during the interview. So Ryan Whitaker Smith and I didn't exactly fit in with our hoodies and jeans, with our open laughter. Nevertheless, it was quiet enough for conversation and a quiet coffee shop is a rare thing these days.

As I turn on my voice recorder, he leans down and speaks into the microphone: "For the record," he says, "I'm a film producer, so I feel very uncomfortable being called a poet."

We laugh. I say, "We're off to a great start. Okay, you have two books of poetry. Tell me about their genesis."

"I had no intention of writing a book for publication," he says. "I didn't think I was qualified. That's not false modesty; it's how I felt. At one point, I rewrote a psalm during my private devotions as a kind of prayer. The psalms are already prayers, so this was more like a poetic rendering. I shared it with my friend and mentor, Dan Wilt, and he found it interesting. We ended up doing several more together, a kind of back-and-forth exchange. By the time it was said and done, we had twenty of these poems which we printed in a little booklet and gave as a gift to friends and family at Christmas."

"What a great idea."

"Well, one of those friends was Carolyn Weber, author of *Surprised by Oxford*. She asked if she could share them with some publishing friends of hers. Without intending to do it, that booklet became a kind of proof of concept which was picked up by a publisher. We initially just wanted to render a few of the psalms, but they asked us to do all of them, so that's what we did. *Sheltering Mercy* was the first, and *Endless Grace* was the second. Now we're working on another one based on the proverbs." He glances around the coffee shop. "I feel very blessed that anyone caught the vision for it."

"Both of those books were written collaboratively," I say, "which is a unique experience when it comes to poets. Most poetry is written in solitude. Was collaboration advantageous? Was it difficult? I imagine it took a great deal of communication and compromise."

"Because it was a byproduct of our friendship, because it happened so organically, it felt right to me. The biggest challenge was making it sound like it was one voice. That's why I assumed the editor role, I suppose."

"I'm assuming that the collaboration brought you closer as friends."

"We don't talk anymore." He laughs. "I'm just kidding. It absolutely deepened our friendship. We did several writing retreats together to finish the work. What a rich experience."

"Was poetry a part of your upbringing?"

"I don't remember writing a lot of poems when I was a kid, but you can't escape poetry when you go to a classical school. I remember encountering John Donne and being impacted by his work. I wrote my thesis on Donne. I love him to this day. Later, I discovered George Herbert. Those two poets were big for me, but I'm no poetry expert. I certainly came from a musical family, so, to me, there's always been a musical relationship between music and poetry. That's not a novel observation.

But I would add that my work as a film producer and scriptwriter overlaps with poetry. There's a cadence, a rhythm, and a pacing to dialogue, to editing a film. I have to ask myself, how long do I hold this particular shot and this character's lines? Does the camera stay on the character for the duration of the line? Does the line overlap with the next shot? Those are important decisions, and they rest on a musical sensitivity." He pauses and takes a drink. "There's also the actual sound of the words. For as long as I can remember, I've always been drawn to language. So even lies that are beautifully expressed are, to some degree, admirable to me. I might fundamentally disagree with whatever is being said, but I can recognize when it is being expressed beautifully. I think of songwriters I loved when I was growing up. Some of their work is flat-out wrong, but I like the song."

"It sounds like you are distinguishing between form and content. The form can be beautiful even if the content is a lie."

"Precisely."

"When it comes to Donne and Herbert, was it their naked encounter with God, their vulnerability, that moved you?"

"I think that's it. You know, I've always been attracted to truth expressed beautifully. In them, I encountered rich, theological truths expressed in a vulnerable and vibrant way."

"Is there a point at which you could see yourself writing something like Donne or Herbert, something confessional that's not rendered?"

"It's quite possible."

"What drew you to film as a creative medium?"

"I drew constantly as a kid. It was the middle of the '80s when Disney's animation really took off. I was at the perfect age to get enchanted by the animation world, so at some point I started making movies with my friends. We ruined home camcorders trying to film underwater. I became enthralled with trying to tell stories with film. My parents actually bought me an editing console that had two VHS decks and you could splice your work together. It looked worse and worse, of course, the more you edited because the tape deteriorated. Anyway, that's how I started falling in love with the medium."

"Did you go to film school?"

"No, I just learned on the job. I'm still learning. I'll always be learning."

"Do you find that the experience of making a film impacted the way you rendered the psalms?"

"Probably. I think there's a relationship between poetry and dialogue. It's all about selection and omission in film, what you show and what you don't show. I think it was Martin Scorsese who said that cinema is all about what's in the frame and what's out. It's the same with writing. You're working within space and time. What are you going to do with the space you've been given? When it comes to writing dialogue in a script, I'm always writing with economy in mind. Poetry is also about the economy of language."

"Many young writers are so caught up in what they're trying to accomplish that they forget about the economy of language."

"I suppose that's probably true in film as well."

"When it comes to rendering the psalms, how did you decide to end your lines? Was it a straight line-for-line decision? Was it the rhythm of the line?"

"There wasn't a unifying filter for those decisions. Each one was different. We kind of let the text speak to us, and we let it dictate those decisions more organically."

"Can we get into the weeds a little bit? What was your workflow?"

"Let's see. I would go through the psalm and separate it into sections based on the idea communicated. Then I would try to write something that captured that idea. Once I had done that, I would try to stitch them all together. Sometimes, you know, one line in the original text was one line in our rendering, but sometimes that one line in the original became ten lines in our poem because it was so pregnant with meaning. We wanted to unpack it a little bit."

"When I talk to other writers," I say, "sometimes they'll tell me that if they aren't writing, they become agitated, a little bit cantankerous. Did you find that the process made you a better person when you were writing?"

"That's probably because writing is their primary creative outlet," he replies. "With my life, writing is only one part of my creative work. I've always got something that requires my creative effort, so I don't feel that way in general. Let's just say that I like to stay busy."

"How does the work of Donne, Herbert, the psalmists—even the work of Ryan Whitaker Smith— minister to a people hammered by societal and personal catastrophe? How does poetry serve people who feel like the world is falling apart around them?"

"I don't know how most people interact with poetry, but for me, when my soul feels heavy, the best thing I can do is go read the psalms. I always find something new. It's about the combination of truth and the beauty of the language; it's about honesty and vulnerability. I think poetry in general can be a comfort to people. Maybe it's the beauty that comforts us, I don't know."

"Do you find that true of the music industry as well? Does a singer climb the charts because she comforts people? You know, the psalmist is crying out to God and we find a kinship in those cries. We feel like the psalmist is articulating something we wouldn't otherwise know how to articulate. Is the fervor attached to a popular singer connected to the fact that she is crying out on our behalf? Maybe she is saying what we don't know how to say?"

"Yes, I suppose there's some of that. But the pessimist in me feels like that's rarely the reason for popularity. I think the difference might be, I don't know, maybe the simplicity of the words on the page. Nobody is wearing a shirt with the poet Luci Shaw's face on it."

"Maybe we should fix that problem." We laugh.

"I guess there's something simple, something very humble, about the written word. It's not as tied to image. I would hope that a singer's popularity is due, at least in some way, to her skill and her vulnerability, but I'm afraid that image and marketing are tied up in it as well, so it gets a little complicated."

"Is part of the problem that many popular singers are actually validating us?" I ask. "I mean, Donne and Herbert don't validate our feelings. We recognize ourselves in them, but they change us somehow."

"Yes, they make us face uncomfortable truths about ourselves. I think it's rare for pop culture to produce something—whether a song, a movie, or a book—that forces us to honestly look at ourselves in the mirror. Is the song shaping our character in a substantive way, in a good way?"

"If you had just a few minutes to say something to Donne and to Herbert, what would you say?"

"That's tough. I feel a little paralyzed by the question."

"Now you can understand why I like asking the questions," I say, "rather than answering them."

"I see that. Okay, let's try this. I guess I would thank them for expressing the truth beautifully. I would say thank you for giving me the words to describe what I lack the ability to describe. I mean, there are phrases from those writers that have never left me. It still amazes me that you can read those guys even today and be moved in our day and age without strobe lights or smoke machines. It's just words on a page, but tears come to my eyes. Those guys never set out to be culture makers, to be famous. They were just trying to be honest with God."

Lord of the Nations (Psalm 2)
by Ryan Whitaker Smith

Lord,
sometimes I am burdened by the politics of earth:
the serpentine plots of the proud;
the ruthless maneuvering of the underhanded
and double-dealing.

They writhe and seethe,
hungry for gain;
swarming like locusts at the harvest,
darkening the sun;
obscuring the Radiance of Your glory.

But then I remember:
You are not threatened by their taunts,
and Your only proper response
is a high and holy laughter;
Your voice thunders from the heavens,
"Hear me, O great ones,
perched and playacting on your thrones:
there is but one King over all;
if you have eyes to see,
see Him lifted him up."

Yes, Lord, I remember;
I call to mind the words of Your promise,
spoken in ages past to a godly king:
that from his offspring You would send Your Son
in the fullness of time
to live and die among us,
bearing the crucible of His cross,
and to rise,
bringing this world up with Him from the grave.

Are not all nations and peoples Your rightful possession;
the ends of the earth Your just domain?

Those who rule in wickedness
will be humbled before You;
the power-hungry back-broken,
tossed into the street to beg for their dinner.

May all who reign and rule seek wisdom;
the proud be humbled;
the powerful bend their knees before Your throne.
May they know their own poverty,
that they might lay hold of the riches of Your grace.

Indeed, the ground is level at the foot of Your cross,
and all who kneel there,
peasant or king,
find rest for their souls.

As for those who resist;
who cling to power with clenched fist—
they will be crushed beneath the heel.
Blotted out.
Expelled.
Forgotten.

For the rightful King returns for His throne,
and blessed are all who are washed in His blood.

JEANNE
MURRAY
WALKER

"I don't believe poetry springs from momentary and unpredictable inspiration. It arises out of solid knowledge of the fundamentals of language and attentive practice. . .I believe poetry is as much the product of hard work and skill as it is of inspirational flash. I figure if I put in the time and practice, eventually the Muses will give me a gift: I will write something better than I know how to."

—*Jeanne Murray Walker*

My eldest daughter, in college at the time, introduced me to Jeanne Murray Walker. I was immediately impressed by Walker's attention to the poetic craft. I wrote to see if I could buy a signed copy of her book, *Helping the Morning*, as a gift for my daughter. Walker gladly obliged. That was the start of our correspondence. When we finally got to enjoy a focused conversation all these years later, it dawned on me that I had never told her how much I appreciated her craftsmanship. I said, "Jeanne, fairly often, I'll read a poem that strikes me as rushed, a little too off-handed. Your poems feel like the work of a craftsman."

"Thank you," she replies. "It probably started with my long habit of practicing the violin, actually. As a child, I was easily bored. Some days, mostly in the summer when I wasn't in school, I would spend four or five hours practicing exercises or working on the cadenzas of the great violin concertos. I learned that to have any hope of performing on the stage required hundreds of hours practicing scales and arpeggios alone in a small practice room. It might also have had something to do with the fact that between the ages of thirteen and sixteen, first my father and then my older brother suddenly died. I did not find the comforting words of my Baptist church helpful. And I did not find English a useful language to discuss any of it. But I did learn that it's possible to use a language other than everyday transactional English to express the truths that go on in and between us. This is the language of poetry and it is often the language of the spiritual world."

"That discipline has remained an important part of your writing career."

"Yes, believe me," she replies, "to get beyond a beginning level, a poet needs to learn craft. When I was teaching in Orvieto, Italy, I got to know a wonderful poet, Hannah Armbrust Badia, who is married to a cobbler. An actual cobbler! He takes measurements of peoples' feet and cuts specially prepared leather and stitches it to fashion mind-bogglingly beautiful—and very, very expensive—shoes. He spent years learning to do this and has dozens of tools in his shop to help him.

He makes shoes; she makes poems. They both spend their days shaping material through hard work and discipline. I don't know whether there is such a thing as an ideal shoe (if there is, it's surely Italian), but I do believe that to make a poem in some ways is not unlike making a shoe. It requires craft and patience."

"I don't think young writers count that cost very often," I say. "I don't blame them; it can look so easy from the outside. But craft involves a lot of study, a lot of time. A lot more than we think it will take."

"I don't believe poetry springs from momentary and unpredictable inspiration," she says. "It arises out of solid knowledge of the fundamentals of language and attentive practice. After reading poetry with careful attention and love for many years, I believe poetry is as much the product of hard work and skill as it is of inspirational flash. I figure if I put in the time and practice, eventually the Muses will give me a gift: I will write something better than I know how to."

"You mentioned the loss of your brother and father. Their deaths must have had an enormous impact on you."

"Those deaths did have an impact on me, of course. I suspect they registered deeply. My father had the kind of heart defect that can now be fixed with a simple procedure, but the surgery was just being invented when my father needed it in 1957. He knew about it and flew to the Scott & White Clinic in Texas for a workup, where he was given a fifty-fifty chance of surviving the surgery. My parents didn't like the odds, and he didn't go back for surgery. And as for my brother, he had been a serious asthmatic from the day he was born. My mother, who was a nurse, kept him alive through her skillful care until he was eighteen. He wanted to go away to school and finally she, who had protected him so long, permitted him to leave her. He died during his first week away at college. My own take on this has always been that we were fortunate to have him as long as we did."

"Did you wrestle with God after their deaths?"

"You know, I never asked whether it was God's fault," she replies. "I'm not even sure what it means to say that something is God's fault. In any case, I don't believe it was those tragedies that caused me to wrestle with God."

"Still, a kind of darkness," I say. "Seamus Heaney wrote, 'I rhyme / To see myself, to set the darkness echoing.' Is that true for you as well? If so, how?"

"I wish I knew what Heaney meant. Maybe he meant that language is actually fairly useless at connecting us to one another or even to our own pasts. Maybe all of us live in a kind of linguistic darkness. But even so, at least when the poet makes a rhyme, she is recognizing and echoing herself from an earlier line. In that way, rhyming offers the poet a way to be in touch, at least with herself."

"You mention rhyming. Traditional forms have been an important part of that exploration for you."

"Yes," she says, "Form has been an enormous ally. I have often felt that, if the Muse is working, the forms of poetry can help me discover what I'm thinking."

"Only if the Muse is working?"

"If the Muse isn't working, just forget it; you'll just have a dead sonnet on your hands. I say this after slowly writing a book of sonnets, *Pilgrim, You Find the Path by Walking*, which came out a couple of years ago. Writing those poems taught me a lot about the language."

"Like what?" I ask.

"Well, let's stay on rhyme for a moment. While helping the poet find words for a poem, rhyme also allows a poet to see what she thinks. That is, in Heaney's words, 'to see myself.' Or to put it another way, the poem, and especially its repetitions, make the poet's own thoughts visible to her as well as to her readers."

"Your work lives in a tension between an ideal version of the world and the uncomfortable, often frustrating reality. Is this partly why you write? To explore possibility and wholeness in a fragmented world? Does that make sense?"

"Yes, I think I know what you're asking," she says. "There are many poets whose work lives in tension between the visionary and reality. At least that's what the reader sees after the poet writes the poem. I'm not so sure that's what the writer was aiming for, though. It may be disappointing, but I don't have any such noble reason for writing poetry—for example, to sustain the possibility of wholeness. When I write, I'm not aiming to sell a point of view like 'wholeness' to the reader. It would be more accurate to say that I am, like the reader, a seeker. I write poetry because I'm fascinated by what the language can do—though that isn't entirely it, either."

"We've talked about the discipline involved in the craft, but does this fascination lead to playfulness, too?" I ask.

"When I first saw someone playing a massive pipe organ with not only a keyboard, but all its knobs and stops and pumping the base pedals, I thought that's the way it is when someone's writing a poem. You *play* the language. It's fun and you're involving the whole complicated language. All the possibilities in English are available to you. The only way I could understand Wallace Stevens, I found, was to think about his poetry that way. His work is deadly serious, but it's rooted in play."

Recalling some of her best poems, I say, "I have always been struck by your metaphors, Jeanne. They arrest my attention. I experience a kind of revelation when I encounter them."

"Thank you," she replies. "Several years ago, after reading a lot of poetry, I began to wonder whether many of the metaphors poets have used—at least in the poetry that has lasted—have worked so well because normal people just regularly think in metaphor. I don't mean that we go around awkwardly decoding the world, thinking 'Oh, I see, a light stands for truth and goodness. And if the light flashes on the shore in a dark night, it means home.' No. Metaphor, that kind of equivalence, works pretty naturally for most of us, and we don't spend a lot of time thinking about it. In other words, maybe it's not the poet who sets up the 'revelation' that one thing equals another. It's always been there and when the poet points it out, people grasp it and say, 'Oh! I see.'

"Speaking of metaphors, one of my favorite lines from your poem, 'Staying Power,' is about how words, left to their own devices, will 'toddle off into the godfire.'"

"I wrote that poem about fifteen years ago for a regular Friday afternoon workshop with my friend, the poet Deborah Burnham. Every week for over forty years, Deb and I have exchanged poems with one another, either on paper or by email. We then spend a couple of hours on Friday talking about our new poems. Her remarks are without exception pointed and they are rarely wrong. On the Thursday I wrote 'Staying Power,' I had been teaching at the University of Delaware, as usual, and as I drove an hour home, I dimly remembered that I needed to write a poem for the next day's workshop with Deb. I didn't have any ready ideas. That fact didn't trouble me, because I rarely ever get an idea for a poem in advance. I'm more likely to find a poem by fooling around with language. I knew I would have a little over an hour to write after I got home before the hungry thundering mob of my family would pull up at our dining room table and demand mashed potatoes and hamburger patties. Believe me," she says, "I wasn't writing as a philosopher or a theologian when I wrote those words. They were a result of playing with language."

"That's an encouraging anecdote," I say. "Sometimes I'm so amazed by the flash insight that comes to some poets and I think that could never happen to me. You're saying that I just need to keep playing with language as part of that slow, patient craft work."

"Exactly. You never know what will come."

"Did you ever consider pursuing philosophy or theology?"

"In college I took a course in philosophy and eagerly wrote about big subjects like the ones you are asking about; and several of my best teachers informed me gently that I was better at metaphor than at abstractions. The philosophers sent me over to the literature department. And after a semester studying literature and writing poetry, I won two *Atlantic Monthly* awards—which certainly validated their assessment. I am a poet and someone who can write essays. I'm not a scholar of religion, philosopher, or psychologist."

"Your line about the 'godfire' lifts the reader into the realm of the transcendent. How does a poet make the leap from lived experience to transcendent revelation?"

"I'm afraid I can't talk very helpfully about how I use lived experience to tell human truths. I can tell you that I don't ever think about getting transcendence down on paper," she says. "There's nothing wrong with doing that, it's just not my gift. I wonder how many good poets these days hope to do that. We tend to write about ourselves, about the way we are caught in time, about our landscape and our houses and our lovers. And from that sometimes the transcendent flashes out. If you want to know William Butler Yeats' poems, you need to learn about the town of Sligo, for example, even if there's a good deal about his poems that transcends Ireland. Think of Denise Levertov, a religious poet if there ever was one. Her poetry is entirely grounded in the particulars of her daily life, and yet her work is shot through with the transcendent. Even four hundred years ago, poets were not writing much about the 'transcendent.' Even John Donne, who was so interested in the transcendent that he later became a divine, seems to have wrenched transcendent revelation out of subjects grounded in the body."

"Is this transcendent revelation a byproduct rather than a causal intent?" I ask.

"I guess what I'm saying is it's not mainly writers who make the leap from lived experience to transcendent revelation, it's readers. It seems to be a normal move for regular people to make one thing stand for another. In the case of any two given objects, the poet may be just the first to point out the connection."

"Which brings us back to metaphor."

"Yes," she says. "Metaphor is the William Carlos Williams red wheelbarrow on which everything depends. The importance of the red wheelbarrow is something a writer absolutely has to learn in order to become a poet.

Grab an issue of *Poetry* magazine and start reading, and you will find metaphor on every page. Using metaphor is part of the discipline of writing poetry. A poet has to talk in terms of objects."

"Your comment about the reader experiencing the transcendence is an interesting one," I say. "I think it was Christian Wiman who said that 'poems are mysterious intrusions, things far greater than things I knew.' Is that why the reader has that experience and not necessarily the poet?"

"Maybe," she replies. "I'm just saying that we probably shouldn't locate the meaning of the poem through the experience of the poet, because we don't know what that experience is. And sometimes the poet doesn't, either."

"It feels to me like your poetry is vulnerable without being confessional. Does the raw confessional poet do us a disservice by being so openly naked about experiences?"

"If a reader thinks she's reading a poet who is doing her a disservice by being too confessional, she should put the book down and find another to read. Far be it from me to set up a rule for what experiences can be talked about in poetry, because different readers probably have different tolerances for that kind of intimate detail. But sometimes a poet who is 'openly naked about experience' can make the image of her raw experience work as a metaphor, which invites the reader into the poem. Think of Theodore Roethke who wrote, 'I wake to sleep, and take my waking slow. / . . . I learn by going where I have to go.' Those lines seem confessional to me, but not raw because they are so resonant as metaphor."

"That's a helpful distinction."

"When I was younger," she adds, "I read and admired the confessional poetry of Sylvia Plath and Anne Sexton and other women American poets who wrote in the mid-twentieth century. They were talking about cultural issues I understood. Perhaps because I've always hung onto my faith, I have never experienced the catastrophic despair those poets seem to have felt. But I must say, in both of those poets, what comes through most powerfully, at least to me, is not their own biographies. Interestingly enough, then there's Emily Dickinson, who intentionally omitted most of the details of her life. Now her biography is being excavated for those very facts."

"Who has given you a helping hand over the years?"

"I owe my writing life to some very wise and generous teachers. I met Helen deVette when I signed up for her creative writing course at Wheaton College in 1962. She submitted my work to *The Atlantic Monthly* competition, which I won. The prize was a summer at

Bread Loaf School of English in Vermont, where I met John Frederick Nims, who became my lifelong mentor. Later, he became the editor of *Poetry* magazine. He meant the world to me, opening many doors. My greatest help, though, continues to be my gifted workshop buddy, the poet Deborah Burnham. The two of us met as PhD students at the University of Pennsylvania and have been workshopping every Friday afternoon for forty-five years."

"Could you talk about your hopes for the next generation of poets?"

"I think the hope is that they will get down on paper the fleeting and astonishing truths of their own generation. Not that truth is different for every generation; it isn't. But truth manifests itself in different ways and I hold my breath waiting for the way the next generation will use form to tell us."

"What pitfalls would you encourage them to avoid?"

"The greatest pitfall, I think, is this: to imagine you can write poetry without reading it," she says. "A lot of people think that way. After all, poetry is short. It sometimes seems effortless. And most poets—like most craftsmen—don't talk a lot about the hard work it takes to make a poem. But imagine a baseball player who hadn't even seen many games and doesn't really grasp why he should. Just imagine. He gets on the field. He's playing shortstop. An easy grounder rolls his way and it bounces through his legs. The fans who don't immediately want to kill him want to get up and leave the game. *You need to know the game.* You need practice. Is poetry any different in that way than baseball or the practice of law or becoming a singer? It's work," she says.

"What are the personal habits you would encourage them to adopt?" I ask.

"If you want to be a poet," she replies, "read every scrap of great poetry you can find in English, going back to before Geoffrey Chaucer. Take your time. When I realized that I needed to do that, I just signed up for graduate English courses, which laid out the great poetry. But you can get hold of an inexpensive history of poetry in a used bookshop. Or sign up for a history of literature course at your local college. As an important side note, if you want to study English at a college or university, you need to dodge literary theory. It has spread like weeds in English departments. Just read the poetry itself and find some friends who are doing the same thing. Get together and talk about it. A shoemaker can't make shoes without learning how they're constructed; so learn how to make poems by studying how they're made."

Staying Power
by Jeanne Murray Walker
*In appreciation of Maxim Gorky at the International
Convention of Atheists, 1929*

Like Gorky, I sometimes follow my doubts
outside to the yard and question the sky,
longing to have the fight settled, thinking
I can't go on like this, and finally I say

all right, it is improbable, all right, there
is no God. And then as if I'm focusing
a magnifying glass on dry leaves, God blazes up.
It's the attention, maybe, to what isn't there

that makes the emptiness flare like a forest fire
until I have to spend the afternoon dragging
the hose to put the smoldering thing out.
Even on an ordinary day when a friend calls,

tells me they've found melanoma,
complains that the hospital is cold, I say God.
God, I say as my heart turns inside out.
Pick up any language by the scruff of its neck,

wipe its face, set it down on the lawn,
and I bet it will toddle right into the godfire
again, which—though they say it doesn't
exist—can send you straight to the burn unit.

Oh, we have only so many words to think with.
Say God's not fire, say anything, say God's
a phone, maybe. You know you didn't order a phone,
but there it is. It rings. You don't know who it could be.

You don't want to talk, so you pull out
the plug. It rings. You smash it with a hammer
till it bleeds springs and coils and clobbery
metal bits. It rings again. You pick it up

and a voice you love whispers hello.

JEREMIAH
WEBSTER

"After death, doctors, lawyers, and politicians will have nothing to do. Poets will be the only ones in the same line of work. It's an enchanting proposition that makes my work now a kind of rehearsal for eternity."

—*Jeremiah Webster*

Rumor has it that Sir Walter Scott coined the phrase "book-bosomed" to describe someone who carries a book at all times. I hope the rumor is true. It's an endearing term. If Sir Walter Scott were still taking questions, I would ask him how to describe someone who carries hundreds of books in his heart. What's the name for someone who has memorized so much and loves so deeply that lines—both ancient and modern—spill out of him unbidden? That's Jeremiah Webster.

He greets me with his characteristically wide grin, and after a few minutes talking about his family, I ask him to describe his relationship to poetry as a child.

"I think I found my way to poetry through the Scriptures. I wouldn't say that mine was a house that was particularly attentive to the poetic tradition apart from the fireside poets like Henry Wadsworth Longfellow and John Greenleaf Whittier, or the poets who graced *Time* magazine, like Robert Frost and T. S. Eliot. My parents understood poetry to be an important inheritance, of course, but not a part of everyday life. But the cadence of language I got directly from my dad, a pastor who worked all week on his sermons and would read them out loud. I have vivid memories of him reading from Ezekiel, Isaiah, and Joshua, accompanied by my mother's violin and her students playing Bach's Minuet 1. That exchange of sound and sense, of language intertwined with music, was a constant in the household."

"The love of language was with you early," I say.

"I have always loved language for its own sake— the beauty intrinsic in the thing itself. It's interesting to see how many poets of the twentieth century were pastor's kids. Even if they abandoned orthodoxy later, they found their music in the cradle of the church. I think it informed much of their poetic sense. Liturgical rhythms certainly helped me find my own voice as a poet. It's an inheritance for which I feel immense gratitude. The gospel—the God spell—is something we should be singing all the time. That's what I hope to capture in my poetry."

"How does the Word inform your poetry? What are the practices that help you inform your poetry in that way?"

"We love what we pay attention to," he says. "My kids know that I love them when I look them in the eye, when I put the phone down and give them my full attention. I think that has deep application to our work as poets. Taking the time to really pay attention. I think of prayer in this way. Why do we close our eyes to pray? It's a defiance of our empirical senses. It's a very public acknowledgment that the material world is not the sum total of reality. You have to shut off the noise to attend to the heavenly realm. At its best, the Christian life should be a way of enchantment and wonder. Jesus is always interrogating what we perceive to be true. 'You say . . . but I say to you.' The Christian life should lead us upward and onward to the beatitude economy where the worldly order of things is disrupted. This is the source of abundant life and I'm trying to capture that in my poetry, to mimic it in some small way."

"Would you say that writing poetry is for you an act of imagining that world in hope?"

"All the time. I'm participating in a discipline that the world says is worthless, lacking utility. It's taking time to pay attention to what the world doesn't value. Too often, the reflexive move with music, with poetry, with art, is to ask where we can buy it. Is it on Spotify? Eugene McCarraher critiques this reality with real precision in *The Enchantments of Mammon*. It's the commodification of communal experience. I think that's deeply problematic. It's an attempt to carry and control something that's immaterial. Poets spend their time and energy on something the world doesn't value, and they do so in faith that the work will have enduring significance. It's a way to preemptively enter the habits of heaven. I write poetry because I can't help myself, and because through it I experience the abundant life that Jesus promised to those who follow him."

"So it sounds like you feel a tension between the market economy and the gift economy. And yet you've had books published. How do you see the value of publication?"

"I think that's an open question," he says. "I will always write poems, but I wonder if they all need to get published. Maybe I'll just write them for my friends. In the past few years, I feel less driven to publish. It's less and less the reason to write. Beyond the good mentoring and editing and the improvement of my craft that comes from getting it out to a wider audience, I'm less inclined to seek publication."

"Is there a way in which technology or publication can help give the gift to a wider audience?"

"I wrestle with that. I mean, Jesus didn't publish. I'm haunted by this reality. The Word that never, to our knowledge, wrote down a word. Would his ministry have been more effective if he had shown up in an era of podcasts and Substack? Is that the most effective way to proliferate the message? I see it as a Faustian bargain. I've been told many times that I need a website; I need to get on social media. It too often feels like self-aggrandizement. I can't take the marketing seriously, myself—that's the Gen-X punk rocker in me. I would rather be with friends sharing poetry than spending my time managing those things. When I weigh the pros and cons and try to consider what the abundant life looks like, it looks more like what you and I are doing right now—like friends talking face to face. Gerard Manley Hopkins names the crisis when he writes, 'Each mortal thing does one thing and the same: / Deals out that being indoors each one dwells; / Selves – goes itself; *myself* it speaks and spells, / Crying *What I do is me: for that I came*.' Is life about being seen and heard, or is it surrendering one's self into the life of God? I think it's the latter. My dad used to say it's better to be known by the nameless few than to be known by the nameless masses. I suppose that's the hobbit in me."

"In 'How To Be a Poet,' Wendell Berry wrote, 'Accept what comes from silence. Make the best you can of it. Of the little words that come out of the silence, like prayers prayed back to the one who prays, make a poem that does not disturb the silence from which it came.' Is that connected to what you're talking about?"

"Yes, one of my professors at Whitworth University said that poetry is a language approaching fruitful silence. A good poem is trying to get to a place where words fail. What does T. S. Eliot say in the *Four Quartets*?

Trying to use words, and every attempt
Is a wholly new start, and a different kind of failure
Because one has only learnt to get the better of words
For the thing one no longer has to say, or the way in which
One is no longer disposed to say it. And so each venture
Is a new beginning, a raid on the inarticulate,
With shabby equipment always deteriorating
In the general mess of imprecision of feeling,
Undisciplined squads of emotion. And what there is to conquer
By strength and submission, has already been discovered
Once or twice, or several times, by men whom one cannot hope
To emulate—but there is no competition—
There is only the fight to recover what has been lost
And found and lost again and again: and now, under
  conditions
That seem unpropitious. But perhaps neither gain nor loss.
For us, there is only the trying. The rest is not our business.

"How scandalous to think that I can write poetry post-William Shakespeare, post-John Donne, post-Emily Dickinson. Are you kidding me? It's a fool's errand. My fear is that all the marketing and promotion of the sovereign self will make us lose sight of what Eliot says: 'There is no competition—there is only the fight to recover what has been lost.' Our work is to try and get back to the garden, to the estate of our first parents. I love the idea that God walked with them in the cool of the day. I want that. My heart longs for that. I'm old enough now to be able to list all the big singers and celebrities from when I was younger and my students don't know those names. They don't care. The only name that persists is the name of Jesus. It's astonishing. In *On the Incarnation of the Word*, Athanasius of Alexandria remarked that if Jesus is dead, why do people continue to encounter him on a daily basis?"

"One of the things that can arise in a community is rivalry," I say. "Envy occurs because we're trying to make a name for ourselves. How do we fight against it? Is it just a matter of being aware that it could be a temptation? We're prone to make sidelong glances, to see where we rank. It sounds like you're talking about a lifestyle that makes rivalry difficult."

"A few years ago, I came into a deep realization of the futility of that pursuit. In my office, I have hundreds of books. I could pull out the bestseller from any given year and I'm amazed at how many of those names have been forgotten. We have to rethink where the meaningful resides, reappraise what endures in the kingdom. What treasures are we storing up in heaven? I haven't arrived anywhere near this place of total surrender, obviously, but I want to get closer. I want something more than the sum total of what self-actualized Jeremiah Webster has achieved."

"Can you elaborate on where you think the meaningful resides?"

"One of the things I like about Christ's parables is that he takes things that are relatively marginalized and easily missed and says God's kingdom resides there—in a lost coin or lost sheep. It's in these very domestic, provincial objects that you're going to find the kingdom. I think we did the New Atheists a favor for a time by propagating the notion that God was simply an über-Marvel version of ourselves. Colossians says he is before all things and he holds all things together. And the book of Acts says in him we live and move and have our being. He is sustaining us by his life-giving Word. This revelation should make us attentive to words and the way our words align with the Logos or diverge from the Logos. The patristics suggest that God is active and present in the world, in contrast to the deistic view that God is absent and has left us to make of things as we will. It's this view of God's intrinsic presence, the notion that he presides over everything, that emancipates my heart and re-enchants the world. It has deeply shaped my poetry of late."

"Do you find that your poems have become intensified by life experience?"

"I think I'm writing with a keener awareness of my mortality. What is it about the intimation of mortality that makes me a better writer? I feel the gravity of middle age. There's an urgency to my writing that wasn't there when I was twenty-two."

"You write in various forms, including free verse. How would you respond to those who favor form poetry over free verse?"

"George Steiner, the literary critic, has a wonderful phrase—nostalgia for the absolute."

"What do you think he means by nostalgia for the absolute?"

"I wonder if people have a nostalgia for a time when poetic form was more reliable, when it was understood by the broader culture. Free verse exploded that reliability.

This is nothing new. What is *poiesis* but innovation? It was a scandal when Dante wrote his comedy in Italian, when Mozart wrote his opera in German, when Samuel Coleridge and William Wordsworth wrote about the everyman, and when Virgil prioritized shepherds over Caesar in the *Eclogues*. These were all innovative decisions. I think we're still in aesthetic recovery from the spiritual wasteland of modernity. I think the world wars were so disruptive to our experience of reality, to what was predictable and reliable. I think they did something to our spirits and to our imaginations. I think free verse is attempting to make sense of that chaos. Eliot showed us how poetry might inhabit a region seemingly inhospitable to lyricism. And I think we're still questing for a music that can meet the discord of our present tense."

"How do we prevent the poems we write in free verse from capitulating to the chaos? There are plenty of poems out there that are, arguably, a chaos of words."

"During my MFA studies, I came to see that the reasons some of my peers were writing were fundamentally different from my reasons for writing. I was writing devotionally. Some, however, employed language to demonstrate, sometimes violently, the meaninglessness of the Logos—and that brought about the death of beauty. I think poetry can be evangelistic in that it can reinvigorate people's sense of the good, the right, and the beautiful, rather than merely adding sound and fury to the void."

"Preserving a sense of beauty in free verse rests heavily on how and when you end a line. So how do you make those decisions as a thoughtful Christian?"

"I try to end my lines at a place where the thought I'm trying to convey comes to a natural close. The syllabics govern some of that as well. The line break is reliably guided by the rhythm I've established. Finishing a line on a strong verb, adjective, or noun is preferable. I also like to use line breaks as a way to set up an expectation and then subvert it, or meet that expectation, but broaden the initial presupposition of a given idea. Enjambment expands the range of the possible. And then there's the way the whiteness of the page is an equal conveyer of meaning, along with the words. I like to think of poems topographically, to see the poem as a kind of geography and allow that geography to communicate as much as the words, or at least provide assistance to the message. One example of this is a poem I wrote after my wife and I experienced a miscarriage. I shaped the poem in the form of a box. It was a kind of cenotaph for us. You know, a cenotaph was for those who lost a loved one out at sea, for those unable to recover the body. I needed some kind of incarnation and all I had was this poem. It became a sort of memorial."

"Christian Wiman wrote, 'My God my grief forgive my grief tamed in language / to a fear that I can bear. / Make of my anguish / more than I can make. Lord, hear my prayer.' Poetry is a way for you to bear grief. You aren't writing it for others; you're writing it for yourself. If it is a blessing to others, great, but writing poetry would still be worthwhile."

"Yes. Poetry is certainly how I negotiate and make sense of the world. I would like to meet the chaos of the world with a song, I think. That's W. H. Auden, right? He writes, 'If equal affection cannot be, / Let the more loving one be me.' That should be the heart's desire of every Christian, to be the more loving one. Poetry helps me inhabit this high calling, by the grace of God."

"The world is full of people who are calloused, disillusioned, and driven by mammon," I say. "They've lost a sense of child-like wonder. I hear you saying that writing poetry, at least in part, is a way to combat that tendency in yourself."

"Absolutely. I take myself too seriously with the best of them. Poetry is how I apprehend the reality that

'Christ plays in ten thousand places.' Hopkins again. Writing poetry can look irresponsible and uncouth in an age of digital liturgies, but it's how I stave off despair and stay curious and wide-eyed. It's a space where I'm so invested in what I'm doing, so awake to what God is doing in creation, that I forget myself entirely. That's where I want to be."

"Do you see this tendency in young writers today? Do you see it in your students?"

"I love to tell the story of a student who entered class one day wearing a beret. I asked her what was up with the beret and she said, 'Well, I'm a poet now.' As if the beret was a magical talisman and by wearing it, she could suddenly write beautiful poetry in iambic pentameter." He laughs. "I wish it were true, but that's just not how poetry works."

"Your story reminds me of something Kate DiCamillo, the author of *Because of Winn-Dixie* and *The Magician's Elephant*, once said. She was told back in college that she was good with words, so she decided that meant she would be a famous author someday. She bought a bunch of black turtlenecks and spent her twenties sitting around and disdaining the world." We laugh. "It wasn't until later that she realized the only way to become a writer is to sit down and write."

"Exactly. Do the thing! There's always a temptation to romanticize it, but we have to write and we have to live in a posture of receptivity. Every encounter is charged with grandeur and we need eyes that see it."

"The poems that I enjoy, the poems that I want to memorize, have that quality about them. They give a flash insight, Vladimir Nabokov's 'picnic, lightning,' that makes it worth the journey. There's an instructive quality to that. It makes the world strange again, in a good way. Good poems expand my apprehension of the world."

"Final question. Tell me about your poem called 'Life Work.'"

"That's a poem in which I explore the idea that after death, doctors, lawyers, and politicians will have nothing to do. Poets will be the only ones in the same line of work. It's an enchanting proposition that makes my work now a kind of rehearsal for eternity."

De Anima (On the Soul)
by Jeremiah Webster

With no liturgy
and no word from grieving parents,
my son scans the obituary page
of *The Seattle Times* for news
of Oliver's death.

This is how he mourns a friend
with no pyre for the body,
no processional, or last-ditch libation
to gods who scuttle beneath
the waves of the Acheron
with its cold and constant dark.

The traffic of commerce,
the mounting up of illiterate men,
and the Faustian distraction
of our devices tempts
nihil anima
to take root
in the soiled-state
of our present tense.

I go to Adoration
where silence
accommodates
the wounded God
my son must wrestle past
the aftermath of Covid
and a godless Christendom
in order to see.

I stare at the tabernacle
until the Host becomes
the sealed cave of Lazarus,
a preemptive Sunday,
praying beyond mortal hope,
beyond the absence of saints
not found in *The Seattle Times*,
to see Oliver emerge
among the dead
now living.

MISCHA WILLETT

"I know I sound silly, but whenever I finish a poem, I stand up from this table and clap my hands and charge out to tell someone, 'Hey! Is anyone around? You'll never believe what just happened in there! It happened! Lightning! It was dead, now it's alive. They were just words and now there's a poem."

—*Mischa Willett*

W e met at a coffee shop because Mischa Willett was worried that kids spilling Cheerios during the interview might be a bit distracting. I told him that after raising five children, I would feel right at home. So by way of compromise, I suppose, he brought his effervescent wife and three kids with him to the interview. Unfortunately, Two Kick Coffee, a converted motorcycle shop, was closing. We bought drinks and walked the three blocks to his office on campus, his family veering off to enter their house nearby.

Willett's office was once a dorm room. Now, the cinder-block walls are lined with shelves weighed down by books. We sat down at the round table where I was immediately distracted by the beautiful volume *A House Called Tomorrow: Fifty Years of Poetry*, published by Copper Canyon Press. And next to it, the work of Philip James Bailey, whose influence on Walt Whitman was unfathomable and who wrote the single most-read poem of the nineteenth century, "Festus."

Already we were immersed in words, surrounded by them, swimming in them, admiring them. Mischa's boyish delight in poetry was striking, even contagious.

"Mischa," I say. "There's an urgency and intensity to your writing that I really admire. Your poetry seems to be a response to what's happening around you."

"T. S. Eliot said that each venture is a new beginning, a raid on the inarticulate," he replies. "I think any work that's taking chaos and ordering it is co-laboring with the Holy Spirit. Whether the chaos is the human heart, time and its ravages, or language itself. All of that is holy work, maybe even if it's not done intentionally to the glory of God. It might be glorifying nonetheless because you're doing your human work. And I don't care if you're planting bean rows like William Butler Yeats or making a sonnet, you know."

He pauses. "I guess I'm a romanticist by training, so Percy Bysshe Shelley comes to mind: 'Life, like a dome of many-coloured glass, / Stains the white radiance of Eternity.' We are fragmenting things needlessly, you know what I mean? There's a Word beneath the words that holds everything together. That is real and true, and poetry isn't artificially putting an order on things so you can feel good for a while. That's what it feels like for me in writing. What's that Seamus Heaney poem?

'Digging'? You know, to dig with your little spade toward that wholeness."

"Do you feel like writing is a kind of compulsive digging for you, a continuous digging? At what point would you say you've done your work?"

"That's interesting," he says. "You know, I don't feel my creaturely beat unless I'm writing. If you don't take your dog out for a walk enough. . ." He laughs. "They get a little ornery, but they're totally better after they exercise. That's what writing feels like to me. If I'm not writing. . ."

"And your wife would verify that?"

"For sure! If I'm acting a certain way, she'll say, 'Honey, have you been making anything lately?'"

We laugh. "So there's a kind of self-serving, a good kind of self-serving, in writing," I say. "Writing poetry does something in you and for you, but what can it do for others? How does it serve people who are just trying to survive life?"

"I think it was Franz Kafka who said that literature must be an axe for the frozen sea inside us. I wrote that in my journal twenty years ago. I think the frozen sea is real. The pop singers are crying out, 'Wake me up! Wake me up inside.' People are sort of yelling this into the void. They feel like there's something else, something more, that maybe they are sleepwalking. This isn't a judgment, it's how people feel. I think for me, and for many people I know, poetry has served that function, to suggest the numinous when all they had was a boring phenomenology. I think poetry can be a first inkling of that transcendent order. I mean, there might be a sunset, or a person, or a song that speaks to them with that spark, but. . ."

"Or Balaam's talking donkey?"

"Yes." He laughs. "You can have something that's just a few lines long, but it can change a life. That's crazy. What kind of work is this that we get to do?"

"When you finish a poem, do you feel like you have made this thing? Or do you feel like you have stewarded this thing?"

"That's interesting," he says. "I think of my poems like my children. I know that's common, but as soon as it exists, it exists. It has its own life and its own rights. I'm proud of it in a particular way, but I can't choose which one I like best or which one will impact people the most. I just rejoice that they're out there, and I want people to experience them. I meet so many poets who act ashamed of what they've made and hate self-promotion, but I want to say, 'No, you're not promoting yourself, you're promoting the poem. You made this thing, hopefully for their joy and for their encouragement. Why wouldn't you want to share that?' It doesn't make any sense to me. I know I sound silly, but whenever I finish a poem, I stand up from this table and clap my hands and charge out to tell someone, 'Hey! Is anyone around? You'll never believe what just happened in there! It happened! Lightning! It was dead, now it's alive. They were just words and now there's a poem.'"

"When did poetry awaken you?"

"My parents were teenagers when I came along. My mom was fifteen years old. We were dirt poor and living on food stamps in Arizona. They were intelligent people, but they didn't have time to cultivate the mind. I had four siblings. And we were peripatetic; I moved schools twenty times before I left home. I thought that was normal. I mean, I don't lament it in any way. But there are these snatches of memory: I remember staying in from recess in fourth grade to read poems my teacher had written. What kind of fourth grader stays in from recess to read extra poetry?"

"Yes, I was going to ask if you were in trouble!"

"I know! And what kind of teacher shares her private poetry? I must have shown some unusual interest in poetry to prompt that. Then in around fifth grade I started mowing lawns and getting a little money, which

I spent on books. I would go to garage sales and raid the used poetry books. I didn't know one from another. I bought books and Craftsman tools because I had heard that Craftsman is a really good brand to have. Assuming I would use those tools. But that was it. Not board games or sports, just books."

"The impulse was there from an early age."

"Yes, and I have no idea where it came from," he says, shaking his head."I never saw my dad with a book. Not one time. The television was on all of the time. But I do remember the closest stirring to a literary response was hearing my mother read the King James Bible, which she did fairly faithfully. I remember one time, you know, wearing my footy pajamas, when I wasn't listening to the words anymore. I was leaning into the music of the words. Later, in high school of course, I started writing poetry for girls."

"They're a great motivator."

"Yes, indeed. God has a design."

"What led you to the Romantics and to grad school?"

"I applied to Wheaton College. It was the only school I applied to. I didn't know it was difficult to get into, I just thought, 'That's where I'm going to go.' Here's this kid from the wrong side of the tracks attending school in what was, at the time, the third wealthiest county in America. I honestly don't think I had ever seen a man wearing khaki pants until I got there, and had certainly never met a professor. My parents didn't take me, I just got on a plane with my little suitcase. It was all very foreign to me. I didn't do well, dropped out after the first quarter. Returned home and worked at the mall It was terrible, so I went back, but had an argument with my roommate and dropped out again. Then, one of my professors called me on the phone. This was before the internet, so he had to have hunted down my phone number. He reached my mother, who gave him my work number where I was measuring men's necks for fitted shirts. Then he talked to my manager, who got me on the phone and told me that I should go back to college. He said, 'What are you doing with your life? Get over here.' No one had ever talked to me that way before, so I did."

"Who was that professor?"

"His name was Jeff Davis. He would later become Dean at Wheaton College. He led a trip to Oxford every summer and invited me to join. So I went and, in C. S. Lewis's words, it baptized my imagination. I had never seen people take education and beauty so seriously. We were playing soccer on a beach in Wales one evening, having just spent time at Dylan Thomas's house, when

Davis looked at me with a smile and said, 'This is how I spend my summers.' And I thought, right there, that this guy had figured something out. I knew what my dad's summers were like—exactly the same as his falls and winters—and he complained every time he came home from work. But this guy is doing this right now and it counts as a job? Dude!" We laugh.

"So Jeff Davis taught me Romanticism, where I was assigned to a Percy Shelley presentation group," he says. "I thank God now because, if I had been assigned some other poet, I'm not sure it would have stuck. But Shelley, that was just it for me. I read everything—notes, fragments, letters. I was absolutely ablaze. That lasted through graduate school."

Recalling Shelley's moral failures, I ask, "How do you reconcile a life so squandered? Not just Shelley, but the entire history of literature is full of writers who left a trail of carnage. And yet, somehow, they had the ability to express something transcendent, something beautiful."

"So there's a memorial sculpture of Shelley in University College in Oxford, which is interesting, because he was thrown out of that college. There's this statue of Shelley that is both beautiful and grotesque at the same time. He is fully nude, having recently washed up on the beach from drowning. His body is white marble held aloft by black obsidian angels. But I think it should be the other way around. His heart was as black as all sin, but the angels are using him for good. God is making the most of his gift, almost despite him. And maybe that's what God does with all of us. There's a holiness to the inspiration, though his life was dark. Weirdly, the poets I love most have had that contradiction."

"You write in a variety of styles, but mostly in free verse."

"I write formal poetry—metrical, rhymed, fixed form poetry—only sometimes. But I find it easier to do that than to write free verse."

"How would you respond to Robert Frost's famous critique that writing free verse is like playing tennis with the net down?"

"Ah, well, that one smarts. I like Robert Frost, I respect him. He was not a flippant sort of person." He laughs. "Maybe it's risky to go against Frost. I'll offer a counter argument. Maybe it's akin to abstract painting. Not all abstract art, but the best of it is really compelling to me. The painter's job is to be true to the gestures he has started. He can deal falsely with whatever he's been given by imposing a predetermined order. It's like jazz. Someone starts doing something and even if that someone is you, you can't just do whatever you want next. The best jazz isn't truly free. The musician has an obligation to the other musicians and to the structure suggested, even if it appears at first structureless."

"It seems to me that you're saying—with all due respect to Mr. Frost—that you're playing a different game. It's not tennis at all. To say all formal poetry is like playing tennis is to reduce the poem to something transactional. Is it a misunderstanding of the nature of free verse?"

"Yes. I guess I'm suggesting that free verse isn't really free," he says. "That's why I'm feeling a little bit of resistance. It's not like it's the Wild West. The poems I write have rules that govern them, I'm just discovering them as I go. It's not the same as having no rules. It's crazy to think about, but I'll compose a line and think, 'That's wrong!' What am I talking about? According to whom? I wrote it. I can do whatever I want, but still. I know it's wrong. And sometimes I can't fix it. There's nothing I can do. Sometimes even after fifteen years, I can't fix the problems that I created in it. That means I'm bound to something, some rule. In metered poetry, it is easy to identify problems. It's much harder in free verse. You're building the thing as you're flying it. You're asking, given x—whatever line that might be—what must necessarily follow?"

"Do you find that to be true at the ends of lines as well?" I ask. "Do you find yourself saying, 'I can't end the line there'? How do you make those decisions? I'm speaking here as someone who used to hate poetry and who found free verse horribly random. I can appreciate those who look at a line that ends without a logical reason and wonder what's going on."

"I can, too. Line endings—lineation—is my favorite part of the practice, actually. Not word choice, topics, new poems, or even poem endings. I love the well-placed line break. A line has done its work when it opens onto possibility. When it suggests—I don't know, it feels like Magneto walking out onto the air or something—that if you kept going in this direction, such and such would happen. Sometimes I tell my MFA students, 'That line hasn't earned its existence. You carved it there, you made it. You need to give it more weight to carry, more music, more life.' Someone once said you have to put every word on trial for its life. That's how I think about the poetic line. This is getting down to brass tacks here, but if I end up like the ancient Greek poet Sappho and all that remains of my work are fragments, does that line do enough that it would be worth saving? Regardless of where it goes from here? Then I know that the line has ended."

"Then the following line would earn its weight in relation to the previous line? Meaning that it either reinforces or subverts or turns it in a new direction?"

"Precisely," he says. "As a reader, we come to the end of a line where it launches into ideal space—the white part of the page—and the mind has enough time to try and finish the line. This happens in conversation, too. We try to finish each other's sentences. That's delightful for you, as a reader, to find out whether you were right or whether you were fantastically wrong. If you are wrong enough times, eventually you shut up and listen and let the other person talk. That's a nice place to be. Silenced. Then you just feel held, comfortable."

"You're talking about a paradoxical peace," I say. "There's tension, but also completion or resolution. Is the writing process clarifying to you as well? Do you write to process your life? Is it a release of tension?"

"No, I wish it was," he replies. "You know, I used to be an amateur photographer. This was before digital, so I would spend hours in the darkroom and it was very peaceful. I could lose myself in there, just focusing on how much time has passed. Poetry causes me to worry. It hurts. My hair falls out. I get up in the middle of the night. If I write a bad line, it haunts me. I obsess. I spent eleven years working on my book, *The Elegy Beta*.

Eleven years during which I thought about the poems every single day. It's obsessive; it's probably unhealthy. I would probably have a more peaceful life if I just knocked off writing poetry. But poetry has also given me my greatest aesthetic highs. I feel a debt to poetry for giving me those moments of clarity, beauty, joy."

"If our gifts are meant for community, how do you advise young poets to avoid the poison of rivalry? How do they navigate life as an artist without succumbing to envy?"

"You know, some communities are rife with it. I've been in places where we would rank ourselves, right? We knew who was better than us and we knew who was worse. And everyone was looking sideways—'Who has been published and should I stab them?' It was knives out all the time. But to be in a community of Christians is entirely different. It feels like holy work. I don't know, is it just something that happens among believers?"

"Maybe the purpose is different," I say. "The Christian lens is a different lens. And the Holy Spirit brings harmony."

"Yes, maybe. And maybe just getting yourself off center stage is part of it. If all of us know that we're serving some other Person, then maybe we don't get as anxious. No one is leaping onto the pedestal, so there's a real difference. The best artistic communities on this earth, in any genre, are gatherings of Christians. I know that one hundred percent. I wouldn't have thought that back in the day. I used to be a bit snide about evangelical art—you know, 'It's not that good' and all that—but I no longer think that and I know, for certain, that they're more nurturing and healthy communities."

"What are some of the missteps that young poets are making?"

"Young writers, people who are new to the craft, no matter how old, tend to be impatient. They cobble together a manuscript and think it's ready for publication. I often have to tell them that this thing they think is finished is actually a great start to a poem that they may not be capable of finishing right now. They may not be technically ready. They may not be emotionally ready. They just want to finish it in a week. I write my poems until I can't write them anymore. Then I come back to see if I can finish it. That may be a week, two weeks, a year. Some of these poems on my desk are seven years old. I still don't know what to do with them. Maybe some new things need to happen to me before I can finish. I think playing the long game is the main thing."

"Do you ever find that random events, comments, or quotes come along to help you solve a poem that you're thinking about? As if there's some greater conspiracy to help you finish what you're working on?"

"Yes. That used to surprise me. It doesn't anymore. You know, the world is structured not by a logic, but by a Person. Christ, the heart of creation. This same Person who knows and saved me is the same one who holds the universe together. I don't think it's crazy that events in my life would stack up to help me do the work God made me to do. If there's a Logos and it is one with God and I'm one with God in a certain way, it's not crazy to think that I could leave these poems around and something would come along to teach me to complete the work."

"This has been a fun conversation. We're almost finished. Here's you final question. How would complete the following: "Dear Poet..."

He pauses, then he apologizes for being a bit sentimental. "I feel like a great deal of my work is trying to figure out how to thank people who are dead, who have given me so much," he says with boyish gratitude. "What is my interior landscape without their poems? Whoever else they wrote those poems for, they wrote them for me. Those poems found me. I feel like I owe them for blessing me so much. I want my work and my life to honor their lives and their work. I guess I would simply say, 'Dear Poet, thank you.'"

Echo Chamber
by Mischa Willett

They say about still-life paintings
that they're a dream straining
against their frame's edges,
that they're what we have instead
of the bowl of fruit, gardens,
or, pardon me, the pleasurable
company of ladies. My having
one is meant to prove in some sense
that I could possess them
if I chose to. The reason
I'd picture a tea cup
on the wall is to show a couple
of abilities: one, mine to do as pleases
me. And two, to say
Hey, so what if I am by myself.
I could have someone over for tea.
You think I couldn't have someone
over for tea? I could. See?

JAMES MATTHEW WILSON

"The value of the arts is not that they bring something new into being, it's that we reveal to each other something fundamentally old, something that transcends time altogether. The need for incarnation is important here. It's a Christian term that speaks into every intellectual tradition. We want to see transcendent things incarnated in concrete form. We want to see the truth, and the truth has to have a form in order for us to see it."

—*James Matthew Wilson*

I suppose now is as good a time as any for confession: I read book prefaces. Not all prefaces, perhaps, and not even the entire preface every time, but most of it. The reason is simple. Sometimes the author lets you in on a secret, provides a key that unlocks the rest of the book, and gives you a glimpse behind the curtain. This happened to me when I read the preface to *The Fortunes of Poetry In An Age of Unmaking*, by James Matthew Wilson. In it, he describes a crisis that launched him on a life-changing journey. His crisis with higher education is one that many others are experiencing, so I decided we should start there.

"I think your experience in graduate school is a point of massive concern," I say, "and it's not unique to you. Tell me the story."

"Like many graduate students in the humanities," he says, "I had fallen in love with the two great, conspicuous qualities of the arts and literature. First, that form matters, and, second, that it matters because a work of art can change your life. Those are the two convictions that I had as an aspiring artist in Ann Arbor in the 1990s. And they're probably the familiar convictions of every artist at every point in human history. Then I went to graduate school and found those instinctive convictions looked upon with the 'bemused scorn of a philosophical smile,' to borrow a line from Michel Foucault."

"These fundamentals were viewed as, what, naive convictions?" I ask. "That you hadn't quite grown up yet?"

"Yes," he replies. "Later, after I entered a doctoral program, I encountered the word 'beauty' and sighed like some disillusioned critic whose cold eye could see through everything. And I remember thinking that there was something wrong with this response. And, sure enough, the more I read the great works of the Western tradition, the more uncomfortable I grew with that posture toward beauty. 'Beauty' doesn't appear there as some sophomoric, superficial, naive, or sentimental term; it appears as probably the most mysterious term, a term that points us toward the ineffable mysteries of the world. To paraphrase the Swiss theologian Hans Urs von Balthasar, why is it that the truth excites us with wonder and that when we know the truth, we feel bound to it, we abide in it, and we don't want to turn away from it? Even when it can be a painful truth? Because we feel the truth calling us. The Greeks suggest that truth's attraction is its beauty. That's why, when we finally understand something, we say, 'I *see* what you mean.' Truth appears to the mind as a form (idea) in splendor; and the splendor of form is the earliest definition of beauty. So there I was, some twenty-three years ago, giving that contemptuous smirk at the word 'beauty,' but now I am convinced—more than ever—that thinking about beauty and pursuing beauty is our highest achievement."

"Your pursuit runs contrary to many of your peers in the academy."

"When I attended academic conferences," he says, "I was surrounded by people who, at some point—with all the unselfconscious enthusiasm of youth—said that they loved books, but who had found that their love could only be justified on terms that are rather loveless. They found that they could only sustain love for a certain author as long as they were sniffing out the ideologies and the political webs of power that gave shape to the work. If you had read to them the final paragraphs of *The Great Gatsby* and said, 'Aren't those lines just beautiful?' they would have given that philosophical smirk as if to say, 'Well, that's how I used to think.' I suppose there's a dualistic consciousness at play in most of the people who enter the academy." He thinks quietly for a moment. "They came for the joy, but then they were taught that their joy was only justified if it broke forth, not in continuous contemplation, but in some kind of tributary of a more serious mode of analysis that was not merely aesthetic—it had to be political."

"In one sense," I say, "they're correct—the aesthetic isn't the end, but the beginning, of contemplation."

"Yes, the aesthetic, as the modern person might conceive it—just looking at the form of a work of art in isolation from everything else—can't be an end in itself, not absolutely speaking. But lacking the transcendental language to explain why, they have to engage in a practice that reinterprets the aesthetic form in terms of a political form. What we're actually called to do and what our nature wants to do is to be awestruck by the appearance of a form which leads us, then, to the contemplation of form itself and to the divine and eternal forms. That's just how the human mind works. That's what Plato was describing in his work; namely, that we encounter appearances and the soul immediately springs up to seek what the apparent form conceals within itself, and what it conceals is form's depth, or simply the interior form. Not only that, but it wants to discover what lies beyond the form, that to which the form points. That's the essence of life for rational animals, for human beings who have been endowed with a spiritual intellect. If you can't look at something, stare at it in awe, and then see how it leads you up to the eternal, then you're not just selling the work short, you're not just selling your profession short, you're selling yourself short. So, going back to that personal and professional crisis, that's why I started writing what became *The Fortunes of Poetry in an Age of Unmaking*. It was my way of working through where things went wrong and, more importantly, what could go right again, if we had a decent literary culture and a decent intellectual life."

I'm reminded of something from my childhood. "That makes me think of Mole in *The Wind in the Willows*," I say, "when he takes a break from spring cleaning and decides to go on a walk. Kenneth Grahame writes, 'Tired at last, he sat on the bank, while the river still chattered on to him, a babbling procession of the best stories in the world, sent from the heart of the earth to be told at last to the insatiable sea.' We should be able to delight in what we read," I suggest, "without bringing the intellect immediately to bear upon it and deconstructing it, but seeing how the beauty of the passage carries the soul up to God."

"Exactly," he says. "The important thing here is that the first experience does not justify itself on other terms. It's justifying itself on its own terms, which then leads us deeper in. We're just entering it more fully because we've come to see it in light of its foundation. That's what the intellect is called to do in every situation: to pursue beauty as it points to the divine."

"I heard someone say that the ordering of the three transcendentals—goodness, truth, and beauty—is an evangelical error that focuses on morality first, leaving beauty to show up, as it were, late to the party. He suggested that the proper order is beauty first, then truth and goodness. Is that a helpful distinction?"

"The ordering of the transcendentals is an interesting question and a conversation for when we have more time together," he says. "But my abbreviated answer is that beauty is first and also last. That's one of the ancient Greek insights: being gives itself first in the form of beauty. That is to say that being is, first, an appearance that attracts. So, to use Aristotle's language, we begin with wonder, with a sudden awe before the wonderful found in the world. Some people have said that Aristotelian psychology is about the reduction of wonder to science; that is to say, that we go from wondering about things to knowing about them to knowing their causes. To them, learning is the reduction of wonder to science. But that's not the whole picture, because when you finally get knowledge, the wonder kicks up all over again and carries you to the next discovery. True science understands that wonder leads to knowledge which opens once more to wonder, and so on and so forth."

"We're living in an age of not only anxiety but a lack of wonder. And yet it's so much deeper than that. The opening poems of your book, *Some Permanent Things*, describe our societal state of *ennui*, or *acedia*, which the monastics used to mean listlessness or torpor of the spirit."

"Josef Pieper got to me early," he says. "I love his book *Leisure: The Basis of Culture*, in which he uses the word acedia, which is translated as sloth, but it's not the sloth of mere laziness or lassitude, it's the sloth of unsettledness with one's own existence. For years I read and re-read *Leviathan* by Thomas Hobbes, because he captures the typical modern condition in a way that people live out even if they haven't read the book or heard his articulation of it. The first thing he does is reduce everything to matter and matter's motion. To Hobbes, life is nothing more than a motion of limbs. It's mechanistic. It keeps going and people try to keep it going—hence, our activities—until it stops. In several different ways, he manages to give a whole account of human life without any need to use the language of goodness. It's impossible to call something intrinsically good on his terms, or to say there is Someone Good, a *summum bonum* toward which all things aim in an enduring sense. That aimless business, to Hobbes, is the totality of our existence."

"That's not much of a life."

"He goes on to say that most of us live in fear. We fear anything and everything we do not know. Human life, for Hobbes, is characterized not by our affirming that our lives are good, but that we have our lives and we fear the alternative. We fear death. That allows us to live lives that are, in the words of my friend R. J. Snell, 'jealously guarded and absolutely worthless.' People are anxiously trying to get ahead. They're not trying to get ahead because they seek some ultimate good, but only because they feel death at their backs. They're trying to keep death at bay for as long as possible. Other than that, we're nothing more than wind-up toys gradually winding down until we finally stop. Hobbes was trying to hang the corpse of the world up on a hook, cut it open, and bleed out all the wonder. That was absolutely necessary to him if there was to be political order. He was trying to eliminate everything but the fear of death in order to create a rational society that would keep death at bay for as many people as possible for as long as possible. In that circumstance— which I believe is our circumstance—the very act of wonder is a threat because, in the first place, wonder says there are things you should love for their own sake and, second, because wonder says there are things you should love more than life itself. Wonder becomes an anti-social public enemy."

"And yet, perhaps," I say, "the job of a poet is to awaken us to wonder."

"I was just reading a book by the philosopher Charles Taylor in which he describes those who awaken us to the eternal as *hors du monde*, 'outside the world.' Those individuals in history who were outside the world—like Christ, like Socrates—call society to account. In one sense, every person has the capacity to do that. I think it was John Paul II who said that human beings transcend culture. History seems like a train of necessity, but at every moment, we are capable of a freedom that is fruitful and will shape the world around us. That's how culture and civilization are built. We have a God who transcends all of this and who has called us to love the highest things. That's the subject of the title poem in my book, *Some Permanent Things*. That poem describes those occasional citizens who realize that there's more to this world, who know that somewhere in the collective attic of civilization there's an old battle flag, a symbol of the things that people have known that transcend the world. The defense of permanent things becomes more costly when the one who knows those things experiences isolation and understands the need to stand athwart his age. We're living in an age when the love of what is genuinely permanent seems unintelligible to other people. You may talk about it, but you become like the clown in the town square whom everyone looks at but nobody understands, and so they laugh at him. They may not understand him, but he's still telling the truth."

"The arts seem primed by God's design for this very thing," I say. "For transcending culture and creating a new thing. But when we look at the decay around us in this age of identity crisis, at the literal self-destruction of our sons and daughters, I wonder how the arts and poetry can actually point us back to the permanent things."

"The best response to a culture of death is not to offer another salient critique of the impoverishment of contemporary reality, but to live good lives and to make new work," he says. "The intrinsic fruitfulness of reality is such that it's always waiting to be reformed, renewed, and cultivated. Rooted in natural being is a desire to be fruitful, to multiply, to make new things. Even when we despair, life goes on."

"That's very interesting," I reply. "I'm always amazed at how quickly my work on my property gets overgrown. Life burgeons up. It's an unstoppable force despite obstacles, despite hardship."

"People who accept the natural fruitfulness of being have the capacity to make something new and good. As long as we are not totally dead to wonder, small communities have the possibility of renewing things and starting over. It's so deep in us because it's not just in our human nature, it's actually ontological—it's deeper than anything peculiarly human. It's so deep that we can't actually get away from it."

"That's a compelling idea. Have you written about this?"

"In my most recent book of poems, *Saint Thomas and the Forbidden Birds*, there are two poems that address what we're talking about. In one poem called 'Waking in Dresden,' I talk about this remarkable thing—that even the victims of the Dresden bombing, when they woke up to a city bombed almost to an unfathomable ruin, were even then beginning to think about the new life they would build. Not out of hope, per se, but out of their nature. There's another poem called 'Seeds' that describes a lilac bush that planted itself within the divided trunk of a maple tree. New things just spring up; that's the order and nature of things. People are very unhappy leading atomized, mechanized, Hobbesian lives. We hear the language of despair and mental illness, but we're all seeking actualization, to become more fully real. According to Thomas Aquinas, that's what it means to talk about goodness. One of the important mysteries of being an artist is that I get to make forms that help us to think about other forms. This artificial form called a poem gets to open up onto and speak of the other forms that are in nature and the form that is beyond all forms, the divine mystery. Everything draws us up to the divine, but the fine arts have a special privilege because they are made specifically to draw us to contemplation, to lead us to the heart of things and beyond."

"One of the temptations for artists is self-expression as an end in itself," I say. "That has given rise to a dismissive posture that discards any and all critique and, more than that, discards the older ways in favor of the new and novel."

"Yes," he says.

"The goal seems to have become self-actualization, but that's not the actualization that you're talking about," I add. "You're calling us to a humbler posture that doesn't say, 'I'm the final reality,' but points to something higher, something greater than self, and greater than the common good. You're suggesting that if we bow the knee, then we can call ourselves and others to a transcendent life that begets beautiful art, a life that points us upward and onward."

"That's correct," he says. "The language of self-actualization, as it was popularized in the 1970s, led to a culture of narcissism. We have that with us today as expressive individualism, but that language doesn't acknowledge that human nature seeks to be more fully human. They're not describing real actualization. Real actualization speaks to the potential within the thing itself which assumes a limit, a determination, and a direction, but also the possibility of those things coming into being as a fullness, a full realization, of being. So a giraffe wants to become more giraffey. Humans want to become more human, not more like a giraffe or something arbitrary. The story of Frankenstein reminds us that when we try to deny limits, we end up creating monsters. We live, of course, in an age where we seem to think that our technologies liberate us from every finitude that our forms naturally give to us."

"We think we have creative license to do what we want," I add.

"I direct a Masters of Fine Arts in Creative Writing, but I'm not a huge advocate of the word 'creative.' I prefer words like discernment, discovery, invention, synthesis, and reformulation, because we are always taking existing things to make new things. We're not making things *ex nihilo*."

"My friend Andrew Peterson has said that he's not a fan of the term 'creatives' because every person is made in the image of God and is, therefore, creative. He hopes that term goes away soon, because calling ourselves creatives makes it sound like artists are unique, as if our actualization will be different than everyone else's, but that's simply not true."

"Absolutely. The origin of that term lies in the soul-deadening waste lands of schools of business administration; it is possible to call people 'creatives' only in one of those pockets in the world where nothing genuinely fruitful will ever occur. At best, we're doing sub-creation, as J. R. R. Tolkien put it. The value of the arts is not that they bring something new into being, it's that we reveal to each other something fundamentally old, something that transcends time altogether. The need for incarnation is important here. It's a Christian term that speaks into every intellectual tradition. We want to see transcendent things incarnated in concrete form. We want to see the truth, and the truth has to have a form in order for us to see it."

"And," I add, "it requires that we not only know God's word, but that we accept what God says about us and about ultimate reality. Those are the limits within which we work. It seems that we're trying to break free from those limits maybe, in part, because we don't necessarily know what God actually says, but also because we don't want to know."

"Indeed."

"I would like to shift the conversation here to talk about one of the key aspects of your poetry—an aspect I really enjoy—which is human relationship. Your poems talk about real people in your life, not simply philosophy."

"I would love to talk about that. One of the drawbacks of being the kind of writer I have been is that people are eager to discuss the philosophical side of things, which I'm happy to talk about. . ."

". . .but it's not the whole picture."

"It's really not. What's most important to me is not the philosophy; it's the poems."

"In 'Verse Letter to My Mother,' you describe an interaction in the car with your mother that addresses a struggle that many artists feel. Can you tell us about that?"

"As a teenager, I was declaiming the kind of writer I was going to be, and my mother said that I really didn't have a lot of experience out of which to write anything good yet. At sixteen years of age, I was adolescently upset at her response. I probably had a 'creative' understanding of the arts. I didn't understand that the arts really do come to us from without, that the task of the artist is not to create something new out of whole cloth. It's not, again, really creativity; it's reception, discernment, invention. It's about incarnation."

"But your mother understood."

"What my mother was doing in that moment is an ancient practice associated with mothers that goes back to Plato's *Republic*, if not earlier," he says. "Mothers give us the traditional thoughts and stories, the myths and aphorisms and dispositions that shape how we see the world—our worldview, as some people would call it. What mothers seem to do is teach us how to read the world. Fathers tend to show us how to make things, how to cut a figure in the world. Mothers tend to teach us how to interpret that figure. All the way back to when we are in the womb, a mother's heartbeat is actually helping to regulate the child's heartbeat. The little ways in which our mothers move through the world are often the ways in which we come to perceive the world. From an early age, because we're in their arms or following them around, what they see is what we see and how they see things is how we see them. We may resent it later on, but it's how we begin to read the world."

"That has profound ramifications," I say, "on how we value the offices of motherhood and fatherhood over and against the many offices we tend to pursue. Part of building a good life, it seems to me, requires valuing the home. Married or unmarried, the habits built in the home are inextricable from what we make."

"Yes, these are the foundational offices, the fundamentals upon which we stand. Poets are tempted to think that we have to be inventive, to surprise readers with a new metaphor or a new image that will strike us anew. I was talking to someone the other day who said rather banally that we can't understand Christ as the good shepherd because we hardly have any shepherds anymore. Well, no, I think we do understand the metaphor."

"It's not very complicated; you're right. But maybe we should still have more shepherds."

"I wholeheartedly agree, we *should* have more shepherds."

"Is there any place for poets to shock us into an awakening?"

"Certainly. I think of Gerard Manley Hopkins as one of the great artists in that vein who is trying to shock us with the pied beauty, with the unusual and the grotesque, in order to help us to see the mystery of being and Christ born within it."

"In fiction, Flannery O'Connor would be one of those, too."

"Yes. She's practically my favorite, as far as writers of fiction go. James Joyce, certainly Willa Cather, is up there, too. But one of the things I've tried to do is to show a convincing representation of what it means to genuinely live a religious life—with all of its mundane and domestic aspects—in an age like ours. That pursuit has required that I actually live in a way that embraces those forms in light of eternity and for the sake of others. When we live in a trivial and evanescent way that values the self over everyone else, that thinks only of the present moment and of personal satisfaction, we destroy the form of the family and deprive ourselves of the examples that would help us build a life. In my book *The Strangeness of the Good*, the entire second half is called 'Quarantine Notebook,' fifteen poems in iambic pentameter that recount the first two months of the coronavirus pandemic. At the time, I was trying to remind us of the permanent forms, to show what Christian family life is like, to show what contemporary life can look like if we actually live with the transcendent things in mind, to represent domestic life and the way in which the eternal, the evanescent, and the historical all interweave around the dinner table. Leon Kass talks about this in *The Hungry Soul*. The kitchen table is a place where all the necessities and the freedoms of human life tend to convene and circulate. The poet Brian Coffey also captures this well in his long poem, 'Missouri Sequence.'"

"These mundane and domestic aspects of life have fallen on hard times. How many families sit down at the dinner table to eat anymore? Even when we know that it's important, we face a thousand activities that can get in the way. You're nudging us to recover what matters most."

"Yes," he says. "I hope we can reclaim these ancient practices, these permanent things that point us to God and give meaning to life. I think we can."

Through the Water, by James Matthew Wilson

*He must in some way cross or dive under the water, which is
the most ancient symbol of the barrier between two worlds*
-Yvor Winters

Far back within the mansion of our thought
   We glimpse a lintel with a door that's shut,
And through which all our lives would seem to lead
   Though we feel powerless to say toward what.
It is the place where all the shapes we know
   Give way to whispers and a gnawing gut.

And so, in childhood, we duck beneath
   The waterfall into a hidden cove;
In summer, pass within a stand of pines
   Cut off from those bright fields in which we rove,
Whose needles lay a softening bed of silence,
   Whose great boughs tightly weave a sacred grove.

When winter settles in, and our skies darken,
   We take a trampled path by pond and wood,
And find beneath an arch of slumbering thorn
   Stray tufts of fur, a skull stripped of its hood,
Then turn and look down through the thickening ice
   In wonder at the strangeness of the good.

And Peter, Peter, falling through that plane,
    Where he had only cast his nets before,
And where Behemoth stalked in darkest depths
    That sank and sank as if there were no floor,
He cried out to the wind and felt a hand
    That clutched and bore his weight back to shore.

We know that we must fall into such waters,
    Must lose ourselves within their breathless power,
Until we are raised up, hair drenched, eyes stinging,
    By one who says to us that, from this hour,
We have passed through, were dead but have returned,
    And are a new creation come to flower.

FURThER READING

If Ben Palpant were given the task of choosing his favorite book by each poet (he was), this is the list he would compile (he did). Consider this a launch pad for discovery.

Slow Pilgrim: The Collected Poems of Scott Cairns

In the Unwalled City, by Robert Cording

99 Poems: New and Selected, by Dana Gioia

David's Crown: Sounding the Psalms, by Malcolm Guite

Duress, by Karen An-Hwei Lee

Rose, by Li-Young Lee

One Man's Dark, by Maurice Manning

Ordinary Time, by Paul Mariani

Fields of Praise: New and Selected, by Marilyn Nelson

Still Pilgrim, by Angela Alaimo O'Donnell

A Thousand Vessels, by Tania Runyan

The Generosity, by Luci Shaw

Sheltering Mercy, by Ryan Whitaker Smith and Dan Wilt

Helping the Morning: New and Selected, by Jeanne Murray Walker

Almost Entirely, by Jennifer Wallace

After So Many Fires, by Jeremiah Webster

Elegy Beta, by Mischa Willett

Some Permanent Things, by James Matthew Wilson